A Penis Manologue

One Man's Response to The Vagina Monologues

A Penis Manologue

One Man's Response to The Vagina Monologues

Joe DiBuduo

JOE DIBUDUO BOOKS

Joe DiBuduo

This book is dedicated to my creative writing instructor at Yavapai College who thought the manuscript too crude to be discussed in her class. She required us to read *The Vagina Monologues,* and author Eve Ensler discusses rape and mutilation of women in her book. I felt my instructor was being sexist because when I wanted to discuss men being raped in prison, she thought it too risqué and crude for her class.

When someone tells me "no," I yearn to do it, just to prove I can. I can't help myself. So my instructor telling me "no" resulted in my writing this book.

Contents

Acknowledgments

Thank you to all who participated in discussions or offered critiques or advice as I wrote *A Penis Manologue*. Special thanks to Irene Blinston, Ph.D. for her book cover and interior design, to Kate Robinson of Starstone Lit Services for editing and creative consultation, and to Jonathan Carlyon for his IT expertise.

Foreword

After reading *The Vagina Monologues*, I put together a survey for both men and women. I passed out self-addressed stamped envelopes for the anonymous questionnaire. Everyone that I asked personally agreed to fill one out. Then I uploaded the survey onto my Web site, **www.joedibuduo.com**, and also posted it on Facebook, Craigslist, and **www.cryonicman.com**, the site for my first (and hopefully, soon-to-be published) novel. Then I created a Web site and a blog at **www.apenismanologue.com.**

I expected to get several hundred replies to my survey. Total replies I received: one. I couldn't believe that in this enlightened age men and women wouldn't talk about the penises in their lives.

I asked a guy at my gym if he would fill out the survey, and after he read it he replied, "If you were twenty years younger I'd kick your ass for asking me questions like that."

Shocked, I asked, "Why?"

"Too personal," was his answer.

Expecting to acquaint myself with some open-minded men willing to fill out my survey, I attended a meeting on Men and Masculinity at Prescott College in Prescott, AZ. To my surprise, mostly women showed up to discuss masculinity. They seemed interested to learn what makes us guys tick. Apparently, we men don't talk about how masculine we are, so I don't know how women are going to learn about masculinity without any men willing to share their thoughts. I guess most men feel we already know we're masculine and don't need to discuss our feelings and emotions as women do. If we do, other men will look at us as though we're sissified.

The instructor at this meeting asked us how we perceived masculinity. Several women equated men to an onion because an onion has many layers. The outside layer is hard and tough but the deeper the layer, the sweeter the onion. I thought that was a nice analogy, as men have to be tough on the outside even if their emotions want them to cry or act in some other unmasculine way. After experiencing this reluctance of males to talk about their penises, I figured I'd change the title of my work to *A Penis Manologue*, because I'm the only one expressing an opinion.

A highly educated woman who read my outline implied that I'd portrayed all men as potential rapists because of my statements throughout the story indicating that men think about and need sex often. Having sex is a healthy habit, in my opinion, but I told her that rape has nothing to do with sex—it's all about control. Rape is a crime of violence, not passion. Sex is not the chief thing that motivates rapists, says A. Nicholas Groth, director of an innovative sex-offender program at the state prison in Somers, Connecticut. "Rape is the sexual expression of aggression,"[1] he says.

I personally have never thought about raping anybody even though I've been a horndog most of my life. I can't remember anyone ever saying, "I'd rape her," or "I'd like to rape her," during any group discussion. I've heard men say what they'd like to enjoy doing sexually to some beauty, but never once heard a man talk about raping someone.

When I was researching penis facts, I found information that has changed my entire attitude about sexual trauma. When I began to write my response to *The Vagina Monologues*, I wanted to make the story a comedy. However, once I started researching and saw the horrors of genital mutilation and other practices that go on around the world, in all strata of societies, I became emotionally upset. I'm one of those people who empathize with any type of victim. The thought of getting raped is horrendous to me, and I can't begin to say how I was affected when I learned about genital mutilation.

When I first began to write the text that eventually turned into this book, my intention was to use it in a screenwriting class at Yavapai College. However, when I attempted to read my chapter on prison rape, my female instructor banned the story from the classroom. It was hard for me to believe that a college instructor would find talking about Jolly Jellybeans a taboo subject. Maybe because nobody likes to talk about what goes on in prison. I began to think that for my mental health, I should shelve the project. Living and breathing penises 24 and 7 was getting to me. It seemed like an abnormal subject to devote so much time to. However, when I saw how reticent most men and even a college instructor were to talk about penises, I felt obligated to write about them. So I elected myself to be the official Nookie Probe writer.

Introduction

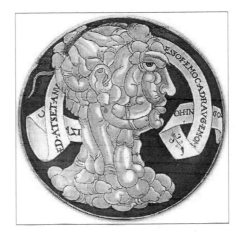

The Ashmolean Museum in Oxford, England bought one of the most celebrated pieces of Italian Renaissance pottery in 2003 for nearly £250,000 and added it to the museum's collection.[1] According to the museum description, this piece is an image of a male head made up of about fifty penises, and was presumably made with an individual in mind. Glazed onto a ceramic plate, the work is thought to have been created by Francisco Urbini in 1536. This goes to show that in those days they knew the penis had a mind of its own, and the image of a guy having his head made from fifty Cockus Erecti probably was meant to show how smart he was. When I became an adult, I realized that a man has two brains—a big brain and a small brain—the one in his head and the one in his pants. I already knew that the small brain generally rules the big one.

Does a penis have a mind of its own? Of course it does. Our small brains control almost everything men do until they reach an age where they become weak and malfunction because our testosterone levels decline. But young men usually think with their genitals. Author and neuropsychiatrist Dr. Louann Brizendine writes in her book, *The Female Brain*, that men think about sex every fifty-two seconds, while women usually only think of it once a day. (The frequency of sexual thoughts and erections are attributable to younger men, not old-timers like me who consider it time to celebrate when the Man Pole raises his tired head.) If men think about sex so often, how do they ever get any work done? How fair is it that men think about it all the time and women less often?

In August 2006, fifty-nine-year-old Oklahoma District Court Judge Donald Thompson was sentenced to four years in prison for exposing himself and using a penis pump and masturbating as he presided over various court cases, including several murder cases. This is a case of penis control over a man's rational mind, and I think, proof positive of the power of the Jolly Green Giant.[1]

I believe the reason men name their male organ is so they won't feel that a complete stranger is making their decisions for them. Not only do men have nicknames for their Mr. Merrymaker, but their wives, girlfriends, and lovers all have a pet name for it as well.

No wonder our penises are confused.

I wondered how many names for the small brain I could collect. Do you know how many penis names there are? Way too many. See Appendix A—Penis Names in Prose. I'll use as many penis nicknames as possible throughout this book to give the reader an idea of the myriad titles for every man's most treasured possession. In fact, my very manly unit is named *Pokey*.

My best friend Pokey is tried and true. He awakens every morning with his head held high. I know he'll continue to be there to guide me through life, and bring me pleasure whenever he can. A friend like this is hard to find; but lucky me, I was born with mine. We treat one another well, and he does all the thinking while I follow. The big brain is under the direction of the small rain, as every man knows. My sympathy goes out to all women because they can never have such a friend. Although I call my friend Pokey, most people call him by his proper name, Mr. Penis.

Penises are what the following pages are all about.

Chapter 1

Penis Replicas

I think it's time to lose our zipper phobia and talk about what's behind the zipper. Is the male organ beautiful, or even pretty? In fourteenth-century Europe, high-ranking noblemen were permitted to display their genitals below a short tunic. Those not impressively endowed wore a fake penis if they chose. These people probably thought their penises beautiful if they displayed them just because they could. I imagine the less well-endowed men made sure their fake penises were beautiful.

Dildos

Our Babymakers must be fashionable if not downright beautiful, because replicas of them are sold worldwide. Many women seem to have a desire to play with a penis of their own. They go to parties, stores, or online to find a penis the size and color they desire. It appears that women have been trying to replace penises with dildos since the beginning of civilization. Dildos in one form or another are found in various cultures throughout history.

The first dildos were made of stone, tar, wood, and other materials easily shaped as penises and firm enough to be used as penetrative sex toys. Modern dildos are made of many different materials and come in all shapes and sizes.

Artifacts found from the high culture era of 10,000 to 40,000 years ago are called "batons" by archaeologists. Some scientists believe the size and shape of these ice age implements leaves little doubt that they were "sex toys." The world's oldest known dildo is a 20-centimeter siltstone phallus, found in Hohle Fels Cave near Ulm, Germany, and is estimated to be 30,000 years old. This dildo was on display at a Blaubeuren museum exhibition.

Dildos were called "olisbos" by the ancient Greeks, who fashioned them out of wood, leather, and stone. Italians in the fifteenth century happily named the toy "diletto," which means *delight* in Italian. The term "dildo" evolved from diletto. Victorian-era doctors created a mechanical portable vibrator to massage female genitals in attempts to cure "hysteria." Were they trying to replace the penis with this invention? Later, the device was advertised in a Sears catalog in 1918.

Even now, there's a harvest and prosperity festival celebrating fertility—Hōnen Matsuri—led by Shinto priests every March 15 in Komaki, Japan. Costumed participants parade a 620-pound wooden penis around Komaki. Throngs of women carry massive dildos in their arms and the food and souvenirs are usually phallus shaped.

The only reason I mention dildos is to point out that no matter how many are created in varying sizes, textures, and colors, the old tried and true flesh and blood, natural-born penis is irreplaceable. But guys, the good news is, we can create replicas of our very own. There are mold making kits out there to replicate your Curious George. There's Clone-a-Willy, Create-A-Mate, and Clone Your Bone. All we have to do is mix the substances in the kits, put them in a super-sized soft drink cup, insert an erect Dingaroo, and wait five minutes. That gives us the negative mold, which we then fill with wax or other soft or hard substances to create a clone of our very own. Once the mold is finished, we can produce as many clones as we want. Think of all the money we'll save at Christmas by giving our girlfriend or wives the part of us they like best.

Chapter 2

Blue Balls

People like to joke about us men being led by our Little Soldiers, but what I'm telling you is true. Penises have ways to control their owners that we never speak about. Like getting so hard and so stiff that the owner can hardly walk, sit, or even sleep without it getting in the way.

Those of you who have never experienced vascular congestion won't understand how if you ignore your Anaconda long enough it'll conspire with the testes to make you so miserable that you have to go hunting for a partner to relieve vascular congestion and prevent the onset of the dreaded blue balls (BB).

BB is the slang term for a congested prostate or vaso-congestion, the condition of temporary fluid build-up in the testicles and prostate region that is caused by prolonged sexual arousal. A pain in the testes usually accompanies the condition. The way to relieve the symptoms of blue balls is through ejaculation.[1] While well known to men, there's scant information in medical literature about BB.

I'll bet most men don't know that women can also experience discomfort due to unrelieved vasocongestion as their pelvic area becomes engorged with blood during sexual arousal. They can experience pelvic heaviness (aka blue walls or blue labia) and aching if they do not reach orgasm. The term *pelvic congestion* refers to pain as it occurs in either sex.

I think there should be a blueballs.com where people suffering BB can go to the site and meet a partner so they could relieve one another, either by practicing online sex or hooking up at an agreed-upon location. If there was such a site, you'd never see me dancing again. Pokey, that little devil, would lose a lot of control if I could easily meet a safe sex partner on the Internet.

As a young boy in school, I hated it when the teacher would call my name and I had to stand beside my desk. Every time, it seemed my Under Thunder stuck out from my crotch as though a tent had been erected in my pants. Pushing Under Thunder between my legs worked for a minute or two, but when I was young, it was so strong that it would soon break free and the tent would form as its all-seeing eye tried to bore through my pant leg. I'm guessing that's why most young men wear jeans today. The heavy material doesn't allow tent making by "you know who."

In those days, there were no surveys and no one admitted they were of average size. All the guys said they were amply endowed with bigger Pleasure Pistons than mine. In 1950, I wasn't a man yet and figured once I could ejaculate, I'd be magically transformed. I did the five-knuckle shuffle with my Weenie every day until I finally ejaculated. I was around eleven and I can still remember that first time. I was lying in bed tenderizing the meat, and when the One-eyed

Gecko burped, the load shot over my left shoulder and hit the headboard.

That young sperm sure was powerful to travel that far. The older I got, the less distance it travelled. I can remember five or six of us doing what we called a circle jerk. We'd all pull out our Jerk Sticks, spank the monkey, and see who could shoot the farthest. The winner got bragging rights until the next contest. A famous American sex educator, author, and artist, Betty Dodson, PhD, thought this behavior perfectly normal. She conducted workshops for more than thirty years in which groups of about ten or more women (and at least once, a group of men) would talk, explore their own bodies, and masturbate together.

Morning Erections

Called Morning Wood in the U.S. and Morning Glory in the U.K., nocturnal penile tumescence is the term used in the urology world. It's all a matter of wet dreams and fantasies during the night—the penis becomes erect in anticipation of a sexual act due to some dream or fantasy. This increased desire to have sex or to masturbate is a good thing for most guys, because frequent erections are good for the health of a Porridge Pump. On average, men experience three to five erections during a normal night's sleep. Erections are the body's natural way of keeping the penis healthy by infusing it with fresh, nutrient-rich blood.

One disadvantage is when you're awakened in the morning by a female relative or if you're in a hurry to leave your home and catch a bus and the erection just won't go away. Morning erections are not at all abnormal and probably are a result of your Gulliver Hard's fantasies. But when you get on that bus, be careful of whom you bump into or you'll be accused of frotteurism—rubbing one's genitals against strangers.

Chapter 3

Use It or Lose It

The tissues of the Big Number One will shrink if you don't stretch them with a normal erection. To keep the body sexually fit, an orgasm every day helps the muscles of your pelvis stay trim, your prostate gland stay healthier, and your sex drive stay stronger. Men who have sex more often live longer than those who don't. Sex lowers blood pressure, reinforces a relationship, and keeps men active. Regular sex seems to protect men from a heart attack and they say that men who have the most sex live the longest.

Frequent ejaculation—whether it happens during sexual intercourse, masturbation, or a dream—isn't likely to increase men's risk of prostate cancer any more than it causes hair to grow from the palms of your hands (an old warning given to youthful masturbators). In fact, new research reviewed by Brunilda Nazario, M.D. suggests it may have the opposite effect and help protect the prostate—apparently, masturbation can be considered a healthy exercise.[1] Next time somebody tells you to exercise more, you know what to do!

Some Penis Facts

Intercourse between a man and woman usually lasts about two minutes. An average woman's orgasm lasts twenty-three seconds, and a man's lasts six seconds. When the man ejaculates, the amount of semen is usually around one to two teaspoons full. An average man will ejaculate 7,000 times in his lifetime and 2,000 of those ejaculations will occur with masturbation. A man ejaculates fourteen gallons of semen in his lifetime. Each teaspoon of ejaculate has about five to seven calories and less than three grams of protein.

Sixty percent of men say they masturbate, and fifty-four percent claim to masturbate at least once a day. Forty-one percent say they feel guilty about masturbating that often. The time needed for a man to regain an erection is from two minutes to two weeks. An average man will have around eleven erections per day, and nine at night.

Men will do almost anything to acquire a massive Muff Mole. Modern science is experimenting with allo-transplants of penises (transfer of an organ or body tissue between two genetically different individuals belonging to the same species). Guess what? Fantasies can come true. An allo-transplant was performed in Guangzhou, China. The patient had sustained the loss of most of his Man Cannon in an accident. Although he gained quite a bit of length and girth, his wife suffered psychologically and insisted that the surgery be reversed. Poor guy, first he loses it, gets a new, improved model, and then his wife tells him he can't keep it. I would've found a new wife who could appreciate my newest addition. Women don't seem to understand that penis size influences men's lives tremendously.

Another manhood fantasy gone real is a lab-grown Maypole. In 2006 researchers succeeded in replacing a rabbit's Wookie with one grown in a laboratory. The penis was grown on a matrix from the rabbit's own cells. Soon we'll be able to grow custom-sized Wing Dings. The term Saturday Night Special takes on a completely new meaning.

Chapter 4

Losing It

Big Dick answers to a part of the nervous system that's not always under conscious control. Sexual arousal usually isn't voluntary. The conscious mind is complicit, but a lot of sexual arousal goes on in the sympathetic nervous system. Therefore, the order for ejaculation comes from the spinal cord, not the big brain, so sexual functioning is affected by spinal cord injury. For men, the main changes are in sensation (or feeling), getting erections (hard), and ejaculating (producing sperm).

Fortunately, men have an advantage over women — we don't need a book to tell us what our penis looks like. In *The Vagina Monologues,* the author describes how some women went through their entire lives without seeing their vaginas. Every man knows he has a Bone Phone, and he's been aware of it and touching it almost from the day he was born. We all know that it has a mind of its own. It takes years of training to stop it from raising its head at the most inappropriate times.

For those of you who aren't familiar with the story, on the night of June 23, 1993, John Wayne Bobbit allegedly raped his wife Lorena. She got a knife from the kitchen while he slept and cut off more than half of his Louisville Slugger. After mutilating her husband, Lorena left the apartment with the severed penis. After driving a while, she rolled down the car window and tossed the penis into a field. John's severed member lay in the field screaming to be reunited with him. Then some poor guy had to pick up the severed organ and bring it to the hospital where two surgeons re-attached it during a nine-hour long operation.

Lorena was found not guilty of malicious wounding by reason of insanity. During and after the trial, Lorena was treated as a feminist hero. "Bobbittmania" copycat crimes were reported around the country and the name Lorena Bobbitt eventually became synonymous with penis removal. If your significant other ever threatens to "Bobbittize" you, cross your legs and hobble away as fast as you can. Lorena could have saved herself a lot of trouble if she would have hired someone to make his Bald-headed Yogurt Slinger disappear.

No kidding, they're out there. I don't know who they are, or how they do it, but a BBC article reported that "members of the evangelical sect, Brotherhood of the Cross, went to the town of Ilesa, Nigeria on 12 April, 2001. The sect members were on a house-to-house preaching mission when someone raised an alarm that his penis had disappeared. An angry mob descended on the visiting evangelists and burned eight of them to death. Two buses and a car were also burned."

That'll teach them to make a man's penis disappear! Then, during September 2003, mass hysteria spread in Khartoum, the capital of Sudan, a situation ultimately quelled by police intervention and statements made by the health minister. The panic was caused by rumors of foreigners roaming the city and shaking men's hands, making their penises disappear. The rumors spread rapidly in text messages on cellular phones.[1]

Penis panics in Southeast Asia are known by the term "Koro." In Chinese, the term used for the condition is shook yang (suo yang, 縮陽). Outbreaks of Koro in China were reported in 1948, 1955, 1966, 1974, 1984, and 1985, although none have been reported in the twenty plus years since.[2]

Chapter 5

Guns and Penises

There are approximately 95,000 firearms per 100,000 people in the United States of America.[1] With all those guns out there, those who say that possessing a gun causes murder may as well say that possessing a penis causes rape.

It's said that American society's problem isn't firearms, but the sexually dysfunctional men and women who abuse them.[2] I wonder if that's true, or if this is a blatantly false statement. Consider that American soldiers during basic training used to recite — with one hand gripping their rifle and the other gripping their penis — "This is my rifle, this is my gun. One's for shooting, the other's for fun!"

We don't need Freud to tell us about phallic symbols. The identification of guns with explosive male sexuality is implicit. Some claim the ownership by females of firearms relates to penis envy, but those same people just might suffer from it, in my opinion. In many instances, I've read that men or women who abuse guns are equally sexually dysfunctional. If this were true, I believe there would be many more women abusing guns than we currently hear about, considering the scores of dysfunctional women I've met!

Females and guns don't mix as often as men and guns, but shooting and hunting organizations for women have become increasingly popular and greater numbers of women than ever are registered gun owners and practice on shooting ranges. Women are trained to use firearms in our military and on our police forces, but crimes in which women shoot people are rarer than cases in which men misuse firearms.

A few well-known women are noted for their gun-slinging skills or their violent use of firearms. Annie Oakley became famous for her expertise with firearms. Calamity Jane's status as a gun-slinger made her a legend. Squeaky Fromme tried to kill President Gerald Ford with a gun and became famous for her crime. Valerie Solanas killed Andy Warhol in a shooting. I'm not sure what the skills or crimes of these women mean in the bigger sexual picture. Maybe Freud was right about his theory of penis envy.

I often wonder what exactly is meant by abusing a gun. Do you deprive it of gun oil—"You've been a bad gun, no oil for you." Or maybe you put it in a drawer and never take it to the firing range. Does not paying attention to it make you an abusive gun owner? I suppose using it incorrectly, as in shooting your husband or your wife is what abuse of a firearm means.

Are the people demanding gun control actually screaming for penis control?[3] Take away a man's guns and he can be controlled. Control a man and by proxy, you control his penis. The next time someone wants to take our guns away and put our penises in servitude we need to ask them these questions: If a car kills five children, do we ban cars or drivers? If a bus crash kills fifteen children, do we ban buses or bus drivers? Each year doctors kill 9,000 patients to every gun death in the U.S., so do we ban doctors? If some idiot goes on a killing spree using guns to kill people, do we ban guns? Makes one see the underlying motivation, doesn't it?

Men and Guns[4]

What is it about men and guns? Is a gun like a penis extender that makes us feel all manly about being able to blow someone's brains out from fifty yards away? Is that manly?

Talking about an extender reminds me of condoms, and the most effective condom ad I ever saw was pictures of fruit with warts all over, symbolic of not using protection. On the other hand, natural, robust, assertive masculinity is defined by some in our society as a disease that must be cured. Being a man used to be so simple. Young males had role models and knew exactly how to talk and act like a man. Today all I ever hear is that men need to become more sensitive. Supposedly, we should be as talkative as women and get in touch with our banal feelings.

I see white, upper-middle-class mothers cling to their whiny sons. The result of this stalls the evolution of masculine identity, which requires boys to leave the maternal nest. Is it any wonder that in the U.S., white male children learn to use guns before they learn to use their penises, while Hispanic and black male children learn to use their penises before they learn to use guns? Don't believe me? Look at the birth rates and see who's using their Hockey Sticks.

Males need to start a penis revolution—burn our jock straps and jockey shorts as the women burned bras in the '70s. Let penises all hang freely in their natural state. No more penis suppression or imprisonments—give them freedom or they'll all be deflated.

It's been proven throughout history that penises are ir-replaceable, so maybe they could go on strike and demand support. Although some may not need support, many do, especially the older ones. Penises need to stand together to demonstrate penis power and demand women support them when requested.

Chapter 6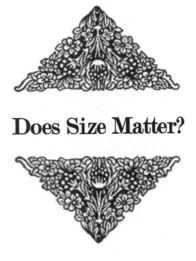

Does Size Matter?

Zamboners come in an array of shapes and sizes. Generally, there are two types. One expands and lengthens when becoming erect (a grower). The other appears long most of the time, but doesn't get much bigger after achieving erection (a show-er). The show-ers are the guys who walk around the locker room without a towel wrapped around their waists. It has been demonstrated that shorter, flaccid penises tend to gain about twice as much length as longer flaccid ones.

Size and Ethnicity

In the 1890s, French military surgeon Dr. Jacobus (the pen name of Jacobus Sutor) found the largest penis ever measured at that time on a "Sudanese Negro": 12 inches by 2 inches. The stunned researcher concluded it was "a terrific machine" and "more likely the penis of a donkey than of a man." He mistakenly concluded that the "Sudanese Negro" possesses the largest genital organ of all the races of mankind." Later studies prove that various penile lengths and widths are found among all races and ethnicities.

Dr. Robert Chartham, PhD (real name, Ronald Seth) measured erect Blue-veined Jackhammers for groups of men of various nationalities for a detailed survey published in 1970.[1] The largest organs for each nationality were as follows: English - 10½ inches; West German - 8½ inches; Negro - 7½ inches; (sic - I have no idea why he used this term when other groups were measured by nationality, not race) French - 7¾ inches; Danish - 8 inches; American - 7¾ inches; and Swedish - 7¾ inches.

The smallest organs in the various nationality groups were as follows: English - 2¾ inches; West German - 3½ inches; Negro - 4 inches (again this is his term, not mine); French - 3½ inches; Danish - 5 inches; American - 3½ inches; and Swedish - 5 inches. There's no mention of India, and it seems the men there didn't want to be measured.

The BBC confirms these sizes with stories stating that a survey of more than 1,000 men in India have concluded that condoms made according to international sizes are too large for a majority of Indian men. The study found that more than half of the men measured had penises that were shorter than international standards for condoms. A range of extra-large condoms has been launched in South Africa, to cater to "well-endowed men." A large number of South African men are bigger and complain about condoms being uncomfortable and too small," said Durex manager, Stuart Roberts. A smaller version is sold in Asia.

"When it comes to size," says Dr. Ciril Godec, chairman of urology at Long Island College Hospital in Brooklyn, "the thing to remember is this: the vagina always adjusts to the penis that's in it."

Size and Identity

My understanding is that a man's weight, build, and height bear no relation to the size of his Colossus in either the soft or erect state, nor are sizes related to foot, hand, finger, or nose size. Art and the media, particularly men's magazines and erotic books and movies, often portray male genitals in "larger than life" dimensions, giving men an unrealistic standard of comparison that can contribute to their concerns about their digit size.

The question is why do many women wish their partner had a larger penis? After a lot of experimentation, I found that women have sexual pleasure centers that need to be physically stimulated in order to achieve orgasm and sexual satisfaction. Women who make love to a man with an insufficiently sized Shaft of Cupid sometimes admit that they're sexually unfulfilled. Sometimes they counterfeit an orgasm. That statement takes precedence over "size doesn't matter." I think that size statement was spread around to comfort the millions of men who have smaller than normal Single-Barreled Pumps.

Women don't usually talk about vaginas and men don't usually discuss the size of our Willie Wonkas, unless they're big enough to brag about. Then we want to show them to everyone who'll look. That may be my opinion, but how many naked pictures have you seen of men with little bitty ones?

I suspected it all along, and believe I'm right. Size does matter. I used to worry about not being able to satisfy a partner with my undersized Nanopud. I was anxious about how I'd compare to other men or my lover's earlier partners. When someone might glance at the Little Guy, I tried to hide him. Having a size that I'm unhappy with has been one of the most frustrating experiences of my life. The largest penis in the animal kingdom is an eleven-foot Boney Cannelloni found on the male blue whale. The female blue whale owns the largest vagina. Gorillas, on the other hand, despite their immense size, have puny organs. They measure just two inches. The smallest natural human penis ever recorded is 5/8th of an inch. That poor guy could never fellatio himself, and he'd probably have a hard time masturbating with only 5/8th of an inch to hold onto. But he could brag that he's almost hung like a gorilla.

But there's hope for these unfortunate men. Surgeons are perfecting a way to build up the size of very small penises to enable proper urination and a full sex life. It's estimated that about one in 200 men is born with what is known as a micro-penis. Whereas the average size of the human penis is around 12.5 cm (5 inches), a micro-penis spans less than 7 cm. In the past doctors have recommended gender reassignment, so these males were brought up as girls, but this is a practice that has ceased in recent years. A University College London (UCL) team has been refining a technique called phalloplasty, or penile enlargement. This involves cutting a flap of skin from the patient's forearm and shaping it into a penis four or five inches long. To maintain erogenous sensation, the original penis is incorporated into the surface of the transplanted skin. Patients receive a urethra to enable them to urinate, and an inflatable penile prosthesis to allow an erection to engage in sexual intercourse.[2]

My Louisville Plugger's size determines who I am and has a huge influence on the quality of my being. It affects my entire existence. I know if I don't measure up, there's always a rubber extender for her pleasure, not mine. I remember way back when it was hard to find sex toys. I somehow got a few French Ticklers, condoms with rubber bumps and squiggly things on the outside that drove my girlfriend wild. They were so rare in the old days that she'd wash them out and powder them so we could use them again. I'm guessing if I wore one of those extenders that fit like a condom with a solid part on top that measures one to four inches, I'd be big enough for most women, no matter what my original size.

There are online sites where you can get a certificate stating that you own the name that you have given your Mr. Clean, and other sites that will generate a name for it.[3] Will Cockus Erecti names be copyrighted so that we'll eventually have to give them numbers, maybe even a tattooed bar code for identification purposes? This might happen in a world where every penis is highly valued and to transplant a bigger one where a small one existed before would be a crime.

Enlargement or Implant?

Lobbyists for the Custard Cannon's industry will probably get that law passed because transplantation will cut into the enlargement business. Statistics are hard to find about how many men respond to all those enlargement ads, but with hundreds of sites advertising online, I'd venture to say a large percentage. After all, our Protein Spigot is what makes us men. The bigger it is, the more confidence we have. I'm sure the enlargement industry is making a fortune selling formulas and promoting enlargement operations. People now are paying for eye color changes, breast enhancements, and many other body image surgeries. I think many men are willing to go through the expense and pain to gain as little as an inch to their Standing Hamptons. Some claims made by the bigger-is-better industry state that by using pills, stretching instruments, exercise, and patches, they'll make your member longer and wider.

If you feel that your Ruby-headed Love Dart isn't big enough, then you're not alone. Despite the fact that most men wish they had a larger Shaft, it is still a taboo subject. Many women are unsatisfied with the size of their partner's Penetrator, yet most would deny it if asked directly, but that's only my opinion. Pokey agrees with me, and smart as he is, I'd say we're correct. This issue has resulted in many men feeling inadequate, and many women feeling sexually unfulfilled. Getting back to size, medical science has determined that the Crack Hunter size is important to a man's self confidence, emotional health, sexual activity, and overall well being.

I call my Man Pole "Pokey" because he always wants to poke someone. He thinks I stunted his growth by not eating the proper diet while he grew. To make up for his phobia about being too small, he wants me to wear shoes two sizes too big. He insists that women always check out my shoe size to estimate how big he is.

If I could have one wish granted it would be that someone invented the Internet in 1950. Why 1950? I was ten years old and my Thrill Drill didn't measure up. If only I could have received the thousands of enlargement ads I now get every day.

The average size for men is 5½ inches, so we're mostly all average, but where are all those under 5½ inchers? Whenever I see a porno flick, the guys always have a footlong Bean Stalk. Maybe I never see the smaller ones because that size is usually hidden. What guy in his right mind is going to show off five inches or less? And what about the unfortunates who are born with micro-penises, or in extreme cases, with a condition called hypoplasia, where the body of the penis is absent and the head is attached to the pubis? I won't even go there!

Chapter 7

Penis Enlargement

Most enlargement procedures come with risks that may not be worth taking. Most men are unhappy with their penis operations. The majority of men who have penis enlargements end up dissatisfied with the results, a study says. *The European Urology Journal* reported that surgeons at St Peter's Andrology Centre in London quizzed forty-two men who underwent operations. The average increase was 1.3 centimeters (0.5 inch), and two-thirds of the patients said they were unhappy with the results.

Understandable when the enlargement ads promise three inches in length and three inches in girth by simply taking their magic formula. One method of surgical "Swizzle Stick enlargement" is to cut the ligament that holds the root of the penis tucked up inside the pelvis and firmly attached to the pubic bone. This operation may give a little extra length if more of the Swingin' Sirloin protrudes from the body, but there are side effects. This ligament, called the suspensory ligament, makes an erection sturdy. With that ligament cut, the erect Ivory Shaft loses its upward angle and it wobbles at the base. The lack of sturdiness can lead to injury. Then again if it's too sturdy, it can break. There is no "Beaver Buster Bone," but the male organ can break. Our Beef Bayonet contains ligaments and cartilage. When a break happens, there's "an audible pop or snap," says Drogo Montague, MD, a urologist at the Cleveland Clinic. The Bayonet turns black and blue and there's terrible pain. It's rare and usually happens to younger men because their erections tend to be quite rigid; enthusiastic masturbation is the most common cause of penile rupture.

Penile Physiology and Embellishment

The Mighty Monkey is constructed of three main areas. One smaller chamber, the lower corpus spongiosum, functions for urination and ejaculation. Two upper chambers, called the corpora cavernosa, are the areas where 90% of the blood is retained during an erection. You didn't know that, I bet, and you probably think this is getting boring. I don't want to be ignorant of how my penis functions, and you men should know this too, just to prove yours isn't the only one with a brain.

To enhance your All-day Sucker you need to develop the size of the corpora cavernosa. Like any tissue of the body, this can be achieved with proper exercises. Not all exercises are effective, and some can be downright dangerous. Traction devices, pumps, and weights have been used with the theory that tissue stretched for a length of time will eventually retain the lengthened level.

There are bizarre practices used by men worldwide to enhance the size of their penises, including the Topinama of Brazil, who encourage poisonous snakes to bite their penises to enlarge them for six months.[1] In Japan, the Yakuza (organized crime) often plant spherical objects under the skin of the penis to increase its size. Asian men have been trying to increase the size of their penises by injecting themselves with Vaseline and other oils. The practice of embellishing the human body by injecting oils beneath the skin has been known for over a century. A man in Britain used a high-pressure pneumatic grease gun to inject his penis. He injected himself with oil to give himself more confidence sexually. But the girth of the man's penis continued to grow and he was no longer able to achieve an erection. Cases of penis enlargement by injection of oils have dangerous side effects.[2]

Clamping is a technique that uses a constricting device, such as a shoestring, cable clamp, or a tight cock ring. Stretching consists of attaching a penis stretcher or "extender" device to it for a set period of time. The device exerts a constant traction on the appendage, which, in theory, lengthens and widens it.

Hanging a weight from the penis is perhaps the oldest self-applied method of enlargement. Over time, the result is similar to the same positive results achieved in Pilates exercises for the body. Then there's the 100% natural way to increase penis length and girth. Jelging is penis milking—no, you don't get milk from your penis, but you do imitate a milking motion to make it bigger. This isn't one of those abundant scams about penile enlargement on the Internet. The method is based on massage techniques that force more blood into the penis. This causes the corpora cavernosa tissue to expand. Men claim that thirty minutes a day of jelging results in tremendous gains. This method is accepted as the most natural penis enlargement process available.

The workout starts by warming the penis up by wrapping it in a towel that has been soaked in hot water. This stimulates blood flow to the penis. Before starting to jelg, lubricate the penis with K-Y Jelly or Vaseline. Once warmed up, start jelging using a grip that completely en-circles the base of the penis, then gently milk towards the head, thus causing more blood to flow there. Two hundred or more strokes make for a good workout. Results are said to be apparent after several months.

Chapter 8

Weird Stuff

How's it hanging? By now, both your brains are spinning and you're ready for some light entertainment. Well, not that kind of entertainment, but I'm happy to share a few fun facts and a real-life tale.

"How's it hanging" is an expression commonly used in the United States as a greeting between friends. I wonder if this phrase didn't come to us from the days of public hangings. When some men were hung, they'd get an erection and ejaculate, shades of autoerotic asphyxiation, the intentional restriction of oxygen to the brain for sexual arousal, a practice that sometimes results in accidental death. But that's serious business for another chapter.

The Caramoja tribe of Northern Uganda tie a weight on the end of their penises to elongate them, sometimes having to knot it up, and the Mambas of the New Hebrides wrap theirs in yards of cloth, making them look up to 17 inches long. If you happen to visit Kenya, you better hold on to your Mister Bojangles. Two Kenyan boys had their penises cut off to make a potion to treat HIV/AIDS. The practice of mutilating the penises of virgin boys is not a tradition, but the object of this mutilation was to "make a potion to cure HIV/AIDS," the BBC article said. Fortunately, they were flown to Spain for successful reconstructive surgery.

When men of the Walibri tribe of central Australia greet each other, they shake Big Macs instead of hands. I can imagine walking into a business meeting with a bunch of Walibiris!

But I'd rather shake penises than partake in the ritual of the Etoro tribe. They're located in New Guinea, on the southern slopes of Mt. Sisa. The young boys of this tribe must swallow the semen of their elders to become powerful adults!

Indigenous people around the world modify their Pocket Otters to enhance their pleasure. There's meatotomy, where one splits the urethra to the base of the glans. Some people split the top of the penis as well to achieve genital bisection. Splitting the glans but not the shaft is known as head splitting. Subincision refers to splitting the top of the penis.[1] Mr. Lifto (a real person) is living proof of how a penis can propel one to fame. His primary claim to fame is the swinging and lifting of weights and objects from his genital, nipple, and other piercings. While many sideshow acts emulate his act, Mr. Lifto can be credited with starting this modern craze.

"Stunt cock" is a term for a well-endowed penis used in extreme close-ups, or when the leading man doesn't measure up or can't get an erection.[2] The stunt cock does the same job a stunt man does. Well not really — it doesn't do dangerous jobs, so I guess "body double" would be a better term.

For the underperformers who don't rise to the occasion, there's a penile injection kit available. The doctor prescribes an injection kit along with the needed drugs. Then the penis is injected with a hypodermic needle in order to get an erection. Poking Pokey with a hypodermic needle to get an erection doesn't seem worthwhile to me, but I guess some guys are willing to do anything for sex.

Three men from Taipei, Taiwan, caused a stir by pulling a wagon loaded with one hundred men for 3 meters by means of cords attached to their penises. With the aid of 17 more penis pullers, they aim to haul a Boeing 747 along a runway using the same method. According to the *Sydney Morning Herald*, the team hopes to break several world records by doing this.

I don't know how true this is, but it's said that King Fatefehi of Tonga deflowered 37,800 women between the years 1770 and 1784 — that's about seven virgins a day. Wilt Chamberlain, the famous basketball player, claimed he had sex with 20,000 women. Most of us don't have access to that many women, or the drive to actually have sex with that many women, even if we fantasize about it.

Here's a real-life tale more typical of us red-blooded American males:

Naked City, 1976

Except for Bob, Chuck the bartender, and me, the Katzenjammers bar on Lincoln Avenue in Chicago's New Town was empty on this beautiful summer day in 1976. I sat there wondering where I could find some excitement when suddenly Bob blurted out, "God almighty, Joe, look at this."

"What, Bob?"

"Na-ked women, by God!"

"Yeah, so what?"

"Goddamn. Take a look."

He shoved a copy of *The Reader* onto the bar in front of me. I took a swig from my frosty Old Style and glanced at a full page ad for the "Miss Nude America Contest." The small print read, *"Get naked and mingle with contest participants during our celebratory dance. Clothing optional."*

"I don't know. What kind of girls would enter a nude contest?"

"Good-looking ones. Look at the paper. It's a nudist camp!"

"Nah, I'm not going. Never wanted to go see a bunch of guys walking around with their Trouser Hawgs hanging out," I said.

Bob looked at me with narrowed eyes. "Who the hell's going to be looking at Pussy Plungers with naked women running around?"

He had a point there, and I didn't have any plans for the day, so I said, "Okay Bob, where is this place?"

"In Indiana."

I didn't know if I wanted to go to a nudist camp with a horndog like Bob. He would screw anything he could get his hands on. I thought of Sally. A nice girl, but a bit retarded. She stopped in Katzenjammers for a beer now and then. Bob took advantage of her every chance he got. Heck, just last week Bob fought with my friend Jack because he'd screwed Jack's girlfriend.

But what the hell. I didn't want to sit in a bar on a beautiful summer day, so I figured Bob could do whatever he wanted once we were there and it wouldn't be any skin off my ass.

"Hey Chuck," I said, "Give me four cases of cold Old Style beer on my account."

"Account, what account?"

"Account of I don't have any money."

Chuck looked at me like I was an idiot. Bob threw a fifty

on the bar.

"Thanks, Bob," I said.

We loaded the beer into my Buick convertible, and I went to the drugstore and grabbed five rolls of film for the camera I always kept in my car. I paid for it. I wasn't really broke, but if I was going to do the driving, I figured Bob could pay for the beer.

I took I-65 to Highway 10 and drove to 3449 East State Rd 10. Near a pale yellow mailbox, I found a sign saying, "Naked City Nudist Camp, next left."

We drank most of one case of beer along the way and got a good buzz going. I almost passed the secluded entrance to the camp, all set back in the woods. We were already on the alert for naked women, but all we could see was nicely-kept round one-story building with a funny sloped roof. Bob and I paid our admittance fee and carrying three beers each, we entered through a gate in the eight-foot high chain link fence surrounding the camp.

"Is this here fence to keep people out, or is it to keep them in?" I asked.

"Hot damn, who cares? They can keep me here for the rest of my life," Bob said, twisting his head from side to side as he kept watch for unclothed females.

We paid our admittance to a big bouncer who allowed us through the gate. Happy as a clam, I couldn't believe I was really at a nudist camp. Never even considered going to one, but here I was. Pokey, my small brain, stood up a little, equally charmed.

"Hot dog!" Bob exclaimed, "sure never thought I'd see so much gash at one time in one place."

It surprised me too, seeing so many shapely women walking around not only topless, but bottomless. I always thought nudist camps were full of older people enjoying the sun. Maybe it was just because of the contest that so many attractive women were in the place. If it was normal for so many lovely women to be prancing around naked, hell, nudist camps would be overflowing with guys like Bob and me.

"Hot diggity dog! Looky there, Joe." Bob pointed to an area where artists were hard at work, painting designs all over nude women.

"Let's go, I always wanted to paint." Bob headed right for the girls.

"Hey! One more step, and you're going to be hurting." A muscular man almost identical to the guy at the entrance blocked our path. Three guys stood behind him, big weightlifters wearing the black T-shirts and jeans that must have been uniforms for security. I grabbed Bob by the arm and pulled him away.

We happily backed off and continued to walk around and ogle the naked women. We stumbled on a stage set up for the girls to parade around on for the contest. A crowd of salivating men with cameras bags and other photographic equipment hanging from their bodies stood anxiously waiting for the contestants. And I mean anxiously. Many of them paced back and forth and anyone could see how worked up they were.

"What's going on with these guys?" I asked a guy who appeared to be more calm and relaxed than the herd.

"Normal behavior for those perverts," he said.

I looked at the camera I carried and wondered if I was perverted for wanting to take pictures. I wanted to ask him, but a roar went up from the crowd. A limo drove slowly towards where we stood.

"That's the owner," the relaxed guy said. "He's a genius. He made a fortune by recruiting shut-ins with nothing to do. He figured a way to have them keep track of radio advertisements in order to assure the companies paying for advertisements received the spots they paid for."

As we conversed, the Lincoln limousine stopped. My jaw dropped when I saw the blonde with size 38-D breasts driving completely nude, and my jaw almost hit the ground when I looked and saw the girl in the passenger seat, a naked brunette who could have been a centerfold model. Pokey went into a spasm when both girls got out.

The loud chatter amongst the leering men stopped suddenly, like someone had turned a volume switch off.

A big security guy opened the rear door of the limo, revealing an interior upholstered with pink fur. A man with leg braces sat there with two additional fine-looking girls dressed in skimpy pink fur outfits matching the car's interior. For him to have women like these attending to him, I figured his attraction had to be money. What else?

"That's him." The calm guy nudged me and pointed to the man who slid out the door and into a wheelchair. "He not only came up with this idea, he opened a truck stop with nude waitresses."

The blond and brunette pulled out a ramp, and the fur-clad girls rolled the crippled genius in his chair down the ramp onto the grass. He looked like he was the happiest man alive and I couldn't blame him. It must be heaven to have so many beautiful women toadying over him. I was almost envious, but I knew I wouldn't trade places with him for anything, no matter how many ladies he had fawning over him.

The loud chattering of men rose again as they oohed and aahed at the combination of the luxurious limo and gorgeous girls. The genius who owned the camp sat smiling in his wheelchair.

Then I noticed some hot babes arriving and strolling into the circular building near the entrance.

"Come on, Bob, let's go get two cases of beer from the

car."

I don't know where I got this idea; I imagine Pokey gave it to me.

"Why?"

"We're going to get inside, where all the hot babes are."

"How?"

"Just follow me." I put a case of beer on my shoulder. Bob followed my example and we went to the door that I had seen the women go through, marked by a large sign that said *Authorized Personnel Only*. I knocked with my left hand as I used my right to balance the case of Old Style on my shoulder. A rough-looking man dressed in the black security "uniform" opened the door.

"Yeah?" he demanded.

"Delivery," I said and pointed to the case of beer on my shoulder. He waved me in, and Bob followed behind with a case on his shoulder. I'd seen stupid stunts like this in the movies, but didn't expect it to work.

Security wouldn't let us get into touching distance while we walked around the camp, but here we were, surrounded by nude females. Pokey got excited, and I knew Bob, horndog that he was, must be going crazy too. The contestants busied themselves with make-up and fixing their hair, the only thing they were allowed to wear in the contest.

"C'mon, Bob, follow me." I found an empty room, put the beer in it, and took off my clothes. Bob started to undress too. "Go find your own room," I said. I didn't want to be naked that close to Bob.

Bob went down the hall. I made sure he stayed in front of me as we walked back to the large open room where the nude contestants congregated. Naked, we fit right in with the crowd. After drinking a few beers and watching the procedure for a while, I noticed when the new contestants came through the door, they didn't know where to go or what to do. Eventually someone would guide them to a dressing room, or should I say, undressing room. Inspired by Pokey, my small brain, I greeted the next girl who walked through the door.

"Hello, I'm Joe. I'm one of your contest judges today. Come with me and I'll show you where to dress, er, I mean, undress."

Bob listened to my line, and emulated me with the next girl as soon as she appeared at the door. I guided the stunning redhead I'd greeted to the room I stored the beer in.

"This is our undressing room," I said out loud. Under my breath I muttered, "Thank you, thank you, God."

She let me help her undress, a miracle to watch a woman who could be the centerfold of the year.

"If I win, I'm using the money to move to Hollywood," she said.

"Are you an actress?"

"What woman isn't?" she said.

"Well, you'll get my vote. You'll probably do well if you go to Hollywood," I said, working hard to keep my eyes on her face.

Even though I was pushing the limits now, I was never a grab-ass type. I always felt empathy for women who I saw being poked and prodded. So I simply reveled being in a room with the best-looking woman I've ever been naked with. The girls got in line once they were ready, so after the redhead got in line, I went to the entrance and guided another new arrival to the room.

"My name is Jean. Are you going to vote for me?" she asked as she unbuttoned her pink blouse.

"Yes," I said.

"Good. I need the money to pay for my son's operation."

"What's wrong with him?"

"Lots of stuff."

I didn't believe a word she said, not even her name. I escorted her out to the main room and escorted a girl with long black hair back to the undressing room.

"How many girls are competing against me?"

"A lot."

She took her jeans, top, panties, and bra off in swift movements and folded them neatly before placing them on a shelf.

"Why are you entering the contest?"

"To show my husband how lucky he is to have me."

I couldn't figure that one out. If my wife entered a nude contest, I wouldn't consider myself lucky.

"You're going to vote for me, right?"

"Oh, of course," I said.

Next, I saw a timid-looking brunette standing by the entrance and escorted her to the undressing room, and found her a spot to leave her clothes.

"Why did you enter the contest?" I asked. That became my first question because I was trying to figure out why women entered these kinds of things.

"The winner is bound to be noticed by the major men's magazines. Heck, I may even make Playboy. Maybe even the centerfold."

Dream on, I thought. She wasn't nearly as attractive as many of the other girls.

Once they let all the spectators in and all the women lined up to stroll on the stage, I stood admiring them, pretending to jot notes on a clipboard I found. One yelled out, "Joe, don't forget, you promised to vote for me." Another said, "He's voting for *me*," and another said, "He told *me* the same thing!"

All of them gave me scathing looks. Pokey shrank from

the humiliation of getting caught lying. My big brain took over at this point, and it didn't let their comments deter me from enjoying the show.

I grabbed my camera and mixed in with the crowd of fully dressed photographers. Once the contest started, the girls pranced artfully around the stage, occasionally bending over this way or that. The crowd of photographers went wild, roaring, pushing, and shoving to try to get closer to take pictures. I couldn't believe the looks on their faces, some hungry, others leering, and every one of them obviously excited beyond belief. I turned my camera away from the women and onto the crowd of men acting as if they'd never seen a naked woman before.

Once the contest was over, Bob and I roamed the camp. I noticed a few other nude men at Naked City. When I saw the sizes of their Towers of Power, I figured they were here mainly to parade their oversized small brains around.

As a man I've been trained to never look at another man's junk, but when it's waved around in the open air, I find it pretty hard not to notice one that's three and four times the size of mine. Pokey didn't measure up to those small brains surrounding me.

Bob and I got to the pool, and by this time we were finishing off the last few beers and drunk as skunks. Otherwise, I never would have had the courage to stand on the diving board and bounce up and down while all the people poolside watched Pokey with derision.

I didn't let it get to me, because I fantasized about the nude dance starting in an hour or so. Unfortunately, I never got to dance. Horndog Bob lost control and grabbed the wrong ass. Security twisted Bob's arms behind his back and escorted us to the gate, throwing us out and our clothes after us.

"If we see either of you in here again, you won't be walking home!" one beefy guy shouted.

"Gawd, this means we're going to miss the dance," Bob said as he pulled his pants on.

For a minute, I thought Bob would bust out in tears and start bawling. I was disappointed about missing the dance too, but exhilarated from the day's events. We got back to my car at twilight. I put the key in and cranked it, and cranked it again. It wouldn't start, but we still had a case of beer. We carried it to the side of the road and drank it while we tried to hitch a ride back to Chicago.

The highway was quiet, but after a long wait, a guy in his thirties picked us up. We introduced ourselves as we climbed into the back seat of his conservative, four-door sedan.

Bob started running off at the mouth. "Holy shit, you should have seen all the putang at the nudist camp."

The driver looked at us in his rearview mirror. "I'm a minister, by the way, and I often wonder why women degrade themselves by doing things like that."

"You'll never figure it out," I said.

"Why is that?"

"From what I learned today, they're all motivated by one thing."

"And what's that?"

Bob leaned toward me, waiting expectantly for my answer.

"They do it because they believe a woman's sense of self-worth is directly tied to her appearance. They'll do any thing, from dyed hair to breast implants and other types of cosmetic surgery to improve their looks and feel better about themselves."

"I wish people could accept the looks God gave them," the minister said.

"I like it when women fix themselves up to look good

for us," Bob said.

I thought about all the women I had met at the nudist camp. "After what I saw today, I thank God I wasn't born a woman."

Pokey stirred his head and agreed with me.

Chapter 9

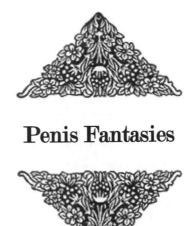

Penis Fantasies

One of my fantasies has always been to invent "Instant Pussy," but not like the stuff that's manufactured now. Everything that's available now is way too complicated. I want my instant Putang Pie to be as easy as opening a pack of sugar. Something that small could be sold over the counter in bars, restaurants, or wherever. Men could satisfy their lust anytime, anywhere. My invention would be created out of some substance that could be packaged like a condom, but when exposed to water it would expand and heat up at the same time. I'd just dunk it in a glass of water and watch as what looked like a chunk of chewing gum unfold and go through a metamorphosis and become the most beautiful and sweetest smelling vagina ever experienced.

A Love Thruster inserted into this device would experience pleasure beyond its wildest dreams. The goop would use nanotechnology in such a way that the instant Cock Sock would almost have a life of its own as it expanded and contracted, heated up, and fit snugly around any size Bacon Bazooker, a feeling so sensuous that any man who used it would never go back to any other organic pussy substitute.

My invention would change the world. Once men discovered how great it was, they'd prefer instant Tuna Pocket to the real thing. I can picture how I'd walk into a bar, order a beer and two instant Hairy Marys, one for now and one for later. No more blue balls for me. My whole focus would change. Instead of searching for an available woman, I could kick back, drink my beer, and watch whatever game was on television. I know it wouldn't last, though. Once women realized the tables had been turned and we didn't need them for sex any longer, they'd become much more aggressive than they currently are.

While I tried to watch the game, all these horny women would try to buy me drinks and ask me to dance. If I agreed, they'd grope me on the dance floor, trying to excite my Ball Buddy. Walking down the street, I'd hear horns beeping and shouts of "Hey, man, looking good!" from horny women of all ages. I'd wish they'd just leave me alone. I'm guessing that's the spot women are in now — they can pick and choose because just about every Beaver Cleaver is looking to hook up. There's so much truth in that old country and western song that says "All the women get prettier at closing time." That would become true for men now. I'd sit in a bar, and at closing time, I'd suddenly be swamped with offers of breakfast in bed and maybe something better. "My day is coming," I tell myself as Pokey draws me out of my fantasy by raising his head when a sexy blonde walks by.

Given a choice of which organ I wanted to donate as transplantable on the back of my driver's license, I volunteered my Sugar Stick, and it coerced me into doing so. It never wants to quit and is always looking to grow. I always imagined a once well-endowed man who lost his Pleasure Missile in an accident and needed a transplant would probably get my Pokey sewn onto him because that was the only organ I gave permission to donate. But once he took the bandages off and saw Pokey, he'd want to sue the doctors.

Sexual fantasies are normal and have a vast range. However, some fantasies can take over one's mind. A gruesome example is that of convicted killer, Armin Meiwes.

Warning - The following fantasy is graphic:

Armin Meiwes, German national, had a really macabre fantasy that he fulfilled. He achieved international notoriety for killing and eating a voluntary victim he had found via the Internet. After Meiwes and the victim attempted to eat the victim's severed penis, Meiwes killed his victim and proceeded to eat a large amount of his flesh. Because of his deeds, he is known as the "Rotenburg Cannibal." Since entering prison, Meiwes has become a vegetarian and has joined a prisoners' group favoring Green Party politics. Do you think he decided he didn't like the taste of penis? I'll bet not one prisoner would let him near their manhood no matter how horny they got. When this guy says "I'll eat you," he's being pretty literal.

Meiwes looked for a willing victim by posting an advertisement on a website called "The Cannibal Café." Meiwes's posted a message stating that he was "looking for a well-built 18- to 30-year-old to be slaughtered and then consumed." Bernd Jürgen Brandes responded. Meiwes is openly bisexual as was Brandes. A videotape the two made when they met on

March 9, 2001 in Meiwes' home in the small village of Rotenburg shows Meiwes amputating Brandes' Dipstick and the two men attempting to eat it together before Brandes' death.

Brandes had insisted that Meiwes attempt to bite his Docking Tube off. This didn't work, so Meiwes used a knife. Brandes apparently tried to eat some of his own meat raw, but couldn't because it was too tough and chewy. Meiwes then sautéed the penis in a pan with salt, pepper, and garlic, but by then it was too burnt to be consumed. Meiwes read a Star Trek book for three hours while his voluntary victim was bleeding to death in the bath. Meiwes gave him 30 sleeping pills and a bottle of schnapps—finally, he then kissed Brandes once and killed him in the Slaughter Room that he had built in his house. After stabbing Brandes to death, he hung the body on a meat hook and tore hunks of flesh from it—he even tried to grind the bones to use as flour. The whole scene was recorded on the two-hour video tape. Meiwes ate the body over the next ten months, storing body parts in his freezer under pizza boxes and consuming up to twenty kg of the flesh.

Web sites have appeared that emulate the one he posted, with people advertising for willing victims. Meiwes is re-ported to have said, "There are 800 'cannibals' in Germany, and they should be treated before they do what I did."

After reading about this guy, my worst fantasies seem safe and tame enough for a children's book. Meiwes, the world's most infamous cannibal, has become a vegetarian. The group Meiwes leads in prison is composed of murderers, pedophiles, and drug dealers.[1]

Freud once stated that only unsatisfied people have sexual fantasies. He was wrong. Studies of human sexual behavior have proven the opposite. Sexual fantasies have been shown to be associated with high libido as defined by high sex drive and orgasm frequency. There is a common belief that men daydream about sex every seven seconds during their waking hours; women more frequently fantasize after they have become aroused. Women who have sexual fantasies during arousal are more apt to experience orgasms than women who do not.

So, don't feel guilty if you find yourself fantasizing about someone who turns you on while you are humping away at your present companion because they're probably dreaming about being ravished by their own fantasy figure, whomever or whatever that may be.

Chapter 10

That's So Gay

To be homosexual means that one is attracted to the same sex. I know you knew that. When I was growing up, I thought the word only applied to men. I wasn't aware there were women homosexuals. When I use the word here, I'm referring to male homosexuals, as lesbians don't have a Cooter Intruder other than the ones they strap on.

In the very beginning of this book, I mentioned how our penises must be fashionable or beautiful because so many women desire one of their own. My theory is that homosexual men fell in love with their old One Eye. Not because he's beautiful, but because he's fashionable. Have you ever met a gay man that couldn't be an interior decorator if he wanted to be?

The rumor is that gay men not only have better fashion sense than the rest of us, but that both their brains are bigger than those of heterosexual men. Maybe the penis brain isn't bigger, but a gay man is said to be endowed with a larger than normal Rhythm Stick. I know that sounds like propaganda, but a report based on data collected by Kinsey in the 1940s reported that, on average, homosexual men had larger penises than heterosexual men. The authors suggest that exposure to male reproductive hormones in the womb may be one explanation.

Gay

Hearing the word *gay* used so much since the turn of the millennium made me wonder how it became a synonym for homosexual. I remember the phrase the "Gay Nineties" and that didn't mean the homosexual nineties. I discovered that the term was originally used until well into the mid-20th century, primarily to refer to feelings of being carefree, or happy. It also came to acquire some connotations of immorality as early as 1637.

In modern English, gay is used as an adjective, and occasionally as a noun that refers to people and practices associated with homosexuality. A new use among younger generations of speakers changed gay to mean stupid as in "that's so gay." Only recently did I discover the younger generation's usage of the word. A college student I knew kept using the term "that's gay," and I finally had to ask what he meant.

Growing up in a working class neighborhood where I couldn't even find a book to read and had to keep my words to four or five letters or I'd be called snooty, homosexual was a word I never heard. The term was simply "queer" and to my friends, queers were put on Earth so we'd have someone to harass and beat up on Saturday nights.

What surprised me is Jimmy Connelly was the instigator of these forays to beat up gay guys in downtown Boston's Bickford's Restaurant where they met up. He hung around with my older brother, so I knew him pretty well. His parents were first cousins, and I always thought that was why he was so weird. Now I know he was a homosexual even back then. Jimmy Connelly's Schlong was so long he could perform fellatio on himself. He happily demonstrated this to anyone who wanted to see. He was influential and we all tried to emulate him. I imagine it would have been quite a sight if an adult came along and had seen a bunch of boys with their legs in the air trying to get their own One-Eyed Trouser Snakes into their mouths. Though many tried, no one else could ever do what Jimmy did. I guess he was pretty unique in his abilities. American biologist Craig Bartle and Alfred Charles Kinsey reported that fewer than 1 percent of men can orally contact their own penises.[1]

Though the *ability* to do autofellatio is rare, what Jimmy *did* wasn't all that unusual. Egyptologist David Lorton said that many ancient texts refer to autofellatio within the religion of Egypt, both in the realm of the gods and among the followers performing religious rituals. According to Lorton, the sun god Ra is said to have created the god Shu and goddess Tefnut by fellating himself and spitting out his own semen onto the ground.[2] To get someone to perform fellatio on their Piccolos was a good thing for the gods.

As nobody else in our group could suck themselves, we were all willing to let Jimmy do it for us. We were all heterosexuals and nobody knew this was considered a homosexual act. Just like those guys in prison think they're normal because they're the doers and not the receivers—my friends all had the same mindset.

Gay, Straight, Pedophile, or All Three?

Phallometry is a word not in common usage, but it should be. There's a penis lie detector, a penile plethysmograph, that is able to pinpoint your sexual persuasion. This is hard to believe, but now I know if I ever question my manhood, I can test it.

You can't lie about what you like and don't like, because the device detects what arouses your Pennis the Menace. This proves the point that it has a mind of its own. Phallometry has been shown to distinguish gay men from straight men. One study showed that homophobic men who have claimed to be heterosexual undergo arousal when given homosexual stimuli.[3]

Pedophilia

Phallometry distinguishes pedophilic men from non-pedophilic men. Bradford's penile tumescence testing on 100 admitted child molesters correctly classified 62 percent of the admitted homosexual child molesters and 52 percent of the admitted heterosexual child molesters he tested. Phallometry can also distinguish men with erotic interests in cross-dressing from non-cross-dressers. Not only that, there is some evidence that phallometry can distinguish groups of men with biastophilia (a paraphilia involving rape) from groups of men without it.

You're probably wondering what this lie detector does. The penile plethysmograph, (PPG) is a controversial type of plethysmograph that measures changes in blood flow in the penis. There are two types of PPG. A volumetric air chamber is placed over the subject's penis, and as tumescence increases, the displaced air is measured.

The circumferential transducer uses a mercury-in-rubber or indium/gallium-in-rubber ring strain gauge and is placed around the shaft of the subject's penis to measure changes in circumference. The band is connected to a machine with a video screen and data recorder. Any changes in the Ball Buddy size, even those not felt by the subject, are recorded while the subject views sexually suggestive or pornographic pictures, slides, or movies, or listens to audio tapes with descriptions of such things as children being molested. Computer software is used to develop graphs showing "the degree of arousal to each stimulus." A roughly equivalent procedure for women, vaginal photoplethysmography, measures blood through the walls of the vagina, which researchers claim increases during sexual arousal.

The circumferential type is more common but the volumetric method is more accurate. The device has been used in Brazil, Britain, Canada, China, Czech Republic, Hong Kong, New Zealand, Norway, Slovak

Republic, Spain, and the United States. The tests have been used in the treatment of sex offenders, in sentencing decisions for sex offenders, as a condition of parole for certain sex offenders. and in some child custody cases to determine if a father is or is not likely to abuse his child(ren). Some psychologists use the PPG to measure the success of the therapy.

Phallometry has also been used to distinguish gay men from straight men—to weed out false gays. One study showed that homophobic men who have claimed to be heterosexual undergo arousal when given homosexual stimuli.

Every male, gay, straight, or otherwise loves his penis, which he keeps hidden from most. On those occasions when he pulls it from his pants, his boy-part bursts forth with high expectations. Usually his Purple-helmeted Warrior is blinded by the urine-stained white porcelain that meets its eye. Regardless of being disappointed repeatedly, he always answers the call in the hope this time it'll see some action.

Our Manacondas are probably the most loyal friends we will ever have. They'll be with us for life, unless we piss some woman off as John Wayne Bobbitt did—a subject that makes me squirm every time I think about it. With all the recent discussion about genital mutilation, I thought Bobbitt's dilemma should be revisited next.

Chapter 11

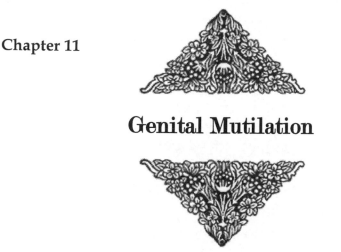

Genital Mutilation

The *Vagina Monologues* discusses female castration in the nineteenth century, performed to stop masturbation. Eve Ensler states, "There are no references in the medical literature to the surgical removal of testes or amputation of the penis to stop boys from masturbating." Evidently, she overlooked circumcision, which is genital mutilation in every sense of the word. During the same era, circumcision was thought to stop boys from masturbating. Circumcision removes three feet of veins, arteries and capillaries, 240 feet of nerves and more than 20,000 nerve endings are destroyed; so are all the muscles, glands, epithelial tissue and sexual sensitivity associated with the foreskin. What is supposed to be an internal organ is changed into an external one.

Circumcision in World Culture

I thought circumcision was only performed on Jews as a religious requirement. It is written in Genesis 17:10-12:

"This shall be the covenant that you shall keep between me and you and your children after you. You shall circumcise all males." Abraham first performed circumcision on himself some 3,800 years ago at the age of 99.

Dumb as I was, I never knew if I was circumcised or not, until one day when I saw an intact foreskin. It looked weird to me. What do people from all of the other countries in the world think when they see our mutilated penises? I'm thinking that a baby boy who is only a few days old and has the most sensitive part of his body cut off without anesthesia probably remembers the pain somewhere in his mind and thirsts to get even with those responsible for taking away part of his penis. We circumcised men only enjoy sex half as much as those not circumcised. The majority of men in the United States and Israel are genitally mutilated soon after birth. I wonder if that's the reason the two countries are such war-like nations. Circumcised men are probably all pissed off and don't know why. I know how much a good kick to the balls hurts, and I imagine getting circumcised equals that pain a hundred times over.

Worldwide, fifteen to thirty percent of males aged fifteen and up are circumcised. The United States has the highest proportion of males circumcised for non-religious reasons, seventy-five percent of non-Jewish, non-Muslim American men are circumcised. Circumcision isn't practiced in Europe, South America, and non-Muslim Asia. Only about fifteen percent of men throughout the world are circumcised. Most parents in the United States are pressured by suggestions to have their sons circumcised after hospital births. The doctor straps the baby down and cuts his foreskin off. How many of us even know what a foreskin is since so many of us have lost it before we even saw it?

Functional or Redundant?

The foreskin is described as a flap of skin on the end of a penis, like a hoody. This implies that the foreskin is something redundant with no real function that can easily be removed with no consequence. This is not the case. The foreskin's length and the fact that it is unattached in the middle allows it to slide up and down the shaft of the penis and roll in on itself over the head of the penis. It is lined with smooth muscle fibers that contract to make the foreskin wrap snugly around the head of the penis. These muscle fibers can relax to permit the foreskin to be retracted. An intact penis has two to three times as much skin than that of a circumcised penis. The foreskin is often long enough to cover the head of the penis while erect, and is extremely sensitive. It is filled with nerve endings called *stretch receptors* that fire when they are stretched, rolled, or massaged. The only purpose of these nerve endings is to make sex more enjoyable. The stretch receptors are unlike the nerve endings in the head of the penis, which are very sensitive to friction but can be so sensitive that the sensation can be irritating or painful. The nerve endings in the head of the penis tend to trigger orgasm much more than the nerve endings in the foreskin.

The head of the penis has no skin. This may surprise those who are only familiar with circumcised penises. The head of the penis is actually covered by a very thin, moist mucus membrane, very much like the inside of the lip or the inside of the eyelid. The head of the penis is not meant to be exposed to friction against clothing, the sun's rays, or soap. It's supposed to be protected by the warm, moist cocoon that the foreskin creates. If the foreskin is removed, the mucus membrane of the penis thickens in response to the lack of protection. It may look like skin, but it is not.

Despite the obviously irrational cruelty of circumcision, the profit incentive in American medical practice is unlikely to allow science or human rights principles to interrupt the highly lucrative American circumcision industry. The medical community should stop participating in and profiting from what appears to be a senseless and barbaric sexual mutilation of innocent children.[1]

Leftover Foreskins

What should doctors do with all those leftover foreskins from circumcisions? Treat the aging population's wrinkles, of course! In the business of vanity almost anything goes. Creams, lotions, and cosmetics are made from many things that most people would be repulsed by. Fish scales in lipsticks, cow placenta in anti-aging products, crushed female cochineal insects in shampoo, and human foreskins are in great demand by the pharmaceutical and cosmetic companies. Valletta is one wrinkle treatment available in the UK that is derived from the foreskins of baby penises. According to *Scientific American,* Valletta uses fibroblasts, cells that produce the skin-firming protein collagen and make elastin, and the source of the fibroblasts is baby foreskins. The fibroblasts in Valletta are isolated from the foreskins taken from baby boys, given several months to grow and multiply in the lab, and then packaged into treatment vials that are shipped to a select group of U.K. physicians. Each vial costs approximately £750 or $1,000, according to the company spokesperson.

Foreskin fibroblasts are used to grow and cultivate new cells that are then used for a variety of purposes. From the fibroblasts, new skin for burn victims can be grown, skin to cover diabetic ulcers, and controversially, it is also used to make cosmetic creams and collagens. One foreskin can be used for decades to grow $100,000 worth of fibroblasts.

Once delivered into the skin, the fibroblasts begin producing collagen, hyaluronic acid, and elastin (which build and reinforce it). They may also make enzymes called *metal-loproteinases* to break down excessive amounts of proteins that accumulate in scar tissue, according to Paul Kemp, Intercytex's chief scientific officer. A nurse from San Antonio said that they have to save infants' amputated foreskins because the hospital's Department of Oral Surgery uses them for reconstructive surgery of the inner lining of the mouth! [2]

A Victorian Practice?

Once I discovered the reason for male genital mutilation, I could hardly believe it. I thought we lived in an enlightened age, but we still practice Victorian-day methods. The American custom has its roots in Victorian Britain at the turn of the twentieth century when doctors began to promote circumcision as a way to prevent masturbation. Queen Victoria started it all because the genealogical tree of the royal family traced their ancestry directly to the House of David, and her descendant, Queen Elizabeth, had her sons circumcised. That's the story all over the Internet, but it may not be true.

During the 1800s, male circumcision emerged as a surgical intervention for "masturbatory insanity" and gained acceptance as a means of desensitizing the penis in order to discourage masturbation. Doctors then believed that masturbation was the cause of insanity, epilepsy, hysteria, tuberculosis, short-sightedness, and death. Good thing they weren't worried about "blow-jobs." Imagine the devious solutions to stopping oral sex. I always wondered where the term blow job came from, because a blow job is actually a suck job. I researched the term on the Internet and found that popular slang has likened the penis to a musical horn or flute since at least the 1700s because someone performing oral sex may look as though they're blowing into a wind instrument.

In 1860, the rate of circumcised males was 0.01 percent. In a doctor's words, the reason for performing circumcision without anesthesia in that era was: "In cases of masturbation we must, I believe, break the habit by inducing such a condition of the parts as will cause too much local suffering to allow of the practice being continued. For this purpose, if the prepuce is long, we may circumcise the male patient with present and probably with future advantage; the operation, too, should not be performed under chloroform, so that the pain experienced may be associated with the habit we wish to eradicate."[3]

In 1935, the medical establishment suggested that all male children should be circumcised. "This is against nature, but that is exactly the reason why it should be done. Nature intends that the adolescent male shall copulate as often and as promiscuously as possible, and to that end covers the sensitive glans so that it shall be ever ready to receive stimuli. Civilization, on the contrary, requires chastity, and the glans of the circumcised penis rapidly assumes a leathery texture less sensitive than skin. Thus, the adolescent has his attention drawn to his penis much less often. I am convinced that masturbation is much less common in the circumcised. With these considerations in view, it does not seem apt to argue that God knows best how to make little boys." [4]

World War II made universal circumcision the standard in the United States. Poor hygiene and desert sand resulted in many cases of severe foreskin infections among soldiers, especially in the North African campaign. Observations by military surgeons convinced them that circumcision protected against certain venereal diseases, particularly syphilis and chancroid (a nasty ulcerating infection of the head of the penis). The foreskin provided a warm, moist environment for dangerous bacterial growth, and the delicate inner surface tore easily during intercourse, allowing infections to enter. By the middle of the war, young recruits were circumcised in U.S. training camps to prevent infections. The American public took heed. By the 1950s, almost all American newborn boys were being circumcised.[5]

In reality, non-religious circumcision is still perpetuated for a number of reasons: ignorance, arrogance, perversion, general disregard for patients' bodies, denial, and, in some countries, profit for the commercially motivated who get paid both for the surgery and for donating the amputated foreskin for research. The profit incentive in American medical practice is unlikely to interrupt the highly lucrative American circumcision industry. The North American medical community should not be allowed to profit from senseless sexual mutilation of innocent children.

The Jewish religious custom of circumcision was probably related to cleanliness in a desert culture with limited water. In later eras, circumcision was used to discourage men from masturbating. By reducing masturbation, circumcision would supposedly cure a range of diseases including seizures, hip trouble, imbecility, paralysis, epilepsy, etc. If that wasn't enough, whenever any new disease became a subject of social concern, circumcision was the theoretical cure. Today it's often said, "If we circumcise Africans, the spread of AIDS will be slowed significantly." I don't know what to think about that. I masturbate even though I'm circumcised, so I'm skeptical about circumcision having any effect on AIDS transmission rates.

Prevention of penile cancer is one reason given for circumcision, but more baby boys die each year from circumcision than men who die of penile cancer. Circumcision does not offer any genuine health benefits, and most Americans view it as benign. It is important to remember that not only the male victims but also society as a whole denies any harm to the boys.

Circumcision removes over half the genital tissue and many specialized nerve endings, thereby killing off sexual sensitivity. Most men are unaware of what they lost. "Sex was always much better with a foreskin," laments a man who was circumcised at age 21 for medical reasons. "After it was removed, it was like going from Technicolor to black and white," he said. Men grow up in some cultures that hold onto old myths about them being innately unclean. It is better to cut away part of a boy's penis than to give someone the task of cleaning it. Another myth is that infant boys don't feel pain, and they require no anesthesia. Fortunately, this attitude is changing and today most American boys receive anesthesia before circumcision. The way males are treated you'd think their bodies didn't belong to them but to some religion or doctor.

In 1994 it was stated that "circumcision causes pain, trauma, and a permanent loss of protective and erogenous tissue . . . Removing normal, healthy, functioning tissue for no medical reason has ethical implications: circumcision violates the United Nations' Universal Declaration of Human Rights (Article 5) and the United Nations' Convention on the Rights of the Child (Article 13)." [8]

Guys don't like talking about any of this stuff, but YouTube is loaded with videos of women talking about circumcised versus uncircumcised penises.[9] Apparently, some women find one or the other more attractive.

Female Genital Circumcision & Genital Mutilation

Feminists decry female circumcisions while somehow believing that male circumcisions are fine. Women's pain is arguably more severe than men's during circumcision.

However, many people, both men and women, disregard the fact that men suffer too.

Female genital mutilations (FGM) are widely reported today and thankfully, the practice is opposed in some areas. Within the past decade, the silence that has surrounded female genital circumcision (FGC) has faded. FGC has become one of the most talked-about subjects among women's groups, especially in Africa. International and professional organizations as well as many governments have recognized that FGC is a violation of the human rights of women and girls. Many communities, governments, and organizations recognize that gender discrimination underlies the practice of FGC and that the most effective strategies for dealing with it involve helping women and girls to become educated and empowered within their own communities and cultures. In addition, these groups recognize that the support of men, community leaders, and other cultures is vital to stopping the practice. Advocacy by women's groups has placed FGC on the agenda of governments and has contributed to the formation of FGC programs, laws, and policies worldwide.[6]

Some of the excuses for FGM are bizarre. In many societies, one important belief is that this procedure reduces a women's desire for sex. Another belief is a women's face becomes more beautiful once she loses her clitoris. Some see the clitoris as a male part. Others believe that if the clitoris touches a man's penis the man will die and others believe that if a baby's head touches the clitoris, the baby will die. Others fear that an uncut clitoris can lead to masturbation or lesbianism.[7]

Feminists against FGM insist that girls shouldn't be mutilated. Of course, I agree with that but women seem to forget that boys are mutilated in the belief that they need an operation before they're normal—circumcision. Male genital mutilation is as serious and has as many negative effects as FGM. But no one talks much about male genital mutilations.

Granted, male circumcision isn't as traumatic as female genital mutilation. Females sometimes have their clitorises removed with a piece of broken glass or a rusty table knife. Most women can't enjoy sex after having their clitoris removed. By contrast, trained doctors or rabbis usually circumcise men under sterile conditions. Men can still enjoy sex after circumcision—actually, they can enjoy half of what they would have if they weren't circumcised.

Chapter 12

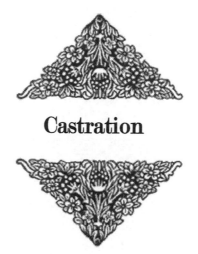

Castration

Somebody mutilated my genitals soon after I was born and now I'm pissed off at the dumbass society that allowed this to happen. I think of all the sex I enjoyed during my life. When I learned it could have been twice as good it upset me. But I can't really complain when I compare circumcision with castration.

The good news is that castration prevents male pattern baldness if done before the hair starts falling. On the other hand, the bad news for captured soldiers in the Middle Ages was that torture by castration was a certainty, and they all knew how painful it would be. Victorious armies probably had little formal knowledge about human physiology, but they knew enough to castrate their victims as slowly as possible to intensify their agony. Every man knows by painful experience that testicles and spermatic cords are both thickly wrapped in nerve fibers and extremely sensitive. In France during the Middle Ages, the castration procedure involved crushing the condemned's testicles in a vise, burst-ting them as mush from the scrotum, and then crunching the spermatic cords with pliers. Not very comfortable for the prisoner hanging by his feet, a position that maximizes blood flow to the brain and makes it nearly impossible to pass out in a state of shock. Overwhelmed with pain and unable to breathe or scream, most castration victims thrashed wildly during and after the crushing of each testicle. The thrashing renewed upon the crushing of each spermatic cord. Perpetrators took hours to accomplish this torture.[1]

In civilizations of old, armies cut off the penises of their enemies as trophies[2], and to make a "head" count of the dead – please pardon the pun! After battles in some cases, winners castrated captives or the corpses of the defeated to symbolize their victory and 'seize' their power, and often to take control of their women. In modern times, the practice still continues – Janjaweed militiamen in the Darfur region in Sudan torture their captives with castration. Over the past decade, at least ninety-four prisoners have undergone the treatment in the Czech Republic, the only country in Europe that continues to surgically castrate convicted sex offenders.[3]

Temporary chemical castration has been studied and developed as punishment and a preventive measure for repeated sex crimes, such as rape or other sexually related violence. A highly questionable permanent chemical castration was Alan Turing's (the father of computers) punishment when he was convicted of "acts of gross indecency" (homosexual acts) in 1952. It is rumored that this resulted in his suicide.

"Voluntary" permanent chemical or surgical castration has been a treatment option for sex offenders in many countries, allowing them to return to the community rather than undergo lengthy detentions. The ethics and effectiveness of this treatment are strongly debated. Physical castration appears to be highly effective as it historically results in a twenty-year re-offense rate of less than 2.3 percent vs. 80 percent in an untreated control group. [4]

The practice of castration has roots in the ancient era before recorded human history. Men have been castrated since the beginning of civilization, it seems. The earliest records for intentional castration to produce eunuchs are from the Sumerian city of Lagash in the twenty-first century BC. Most eunuchs were used as guardians of women or harem servants. Think of those poor guys going through life without any sex drive. What else does a man live for? Yeah, I know, there are other things in life to think about. Coincidentally, the oldest known dildo was discovered in this very city. Is there a relation between castration and women using an artificial Dong Bong?

Castration was frequently used in certain cultures of Europe, the Middle East, India, Africa, and China for religious or social reasons, and eunuchs also staffed harems in several of these cultures. Castration usually involved the total removal of all the male genitalia and posed a great risk of death due to bleeding or infection. In China, castration of a male who entered the caste of eunuchs during imperial times involved the removal of the testes, penis, and scrotum. Preserved in alcohol, the eunuch kept his parts in a pottery jar until the jar was interred with him when he died. Upon rebirth, so the logic went, he could become a whole man again.

In the near future, scientists will be able to construct male or female genitalia from human cells by culturing and growing them over an appropriately shaped lattice or mold. As unbelievable as this sounds, the process of tissue engineering and the ex vivo production of functioning human organs such as the penis and vagina are taking place in the present time. So perhaps in the near future surgically re-moved parts will be grown and reattached. [5]

Ouch!

The testicles make spermatozoa and testosterone. Their removal results not only in sterility but also in loss of testos-terone-dependent characteristics, especially sex drive. His-torically, in some societies these effects were deliberately achieved through the creation of eunuchs, who posed no sexual threat when employed to serve women in harems. Fortunately, for these men, surgical castration involves re-moval of the testes only. When the penis is removed, but the testes are left, a man will still attempt to have sex. How in the hell they do that without a penis is beyond me unless they disagree with Clinton and think fellatio and cunnilin-gus are sexual acts.

If the testes are removed, but the penis left intact, a man is far less likely to attempt to engage in sexual behavior. Removal of the testes generally decreases the desire for sexual activity, rather than affecting the capacity to per-form. These guys have women all around them, and don't even think of sex.

The eighteenth-century Russian Skoptzy sect was an ex-ample of a castration cult in which members regarded cas-tration as a way of renouncing the sins of the flesh. Some followers of a twentieth-century cult, Heaven's Gate, in Rancho Santa Fe, San Diego, were castrated. The group committed mass suicide and nineteen members died at that time, I believe. None of the castrations on the male victims appeared to be recent.[6]

Castrati or Tutti-Frutti?

In Europe, when women were not permitted to sing in church or cathedral choirs in the Roman Catholic Church, boys were sometimes castrated to prevent their voices breaking at puberty and to develop a special high voice. A castrato is a man with a singing voice equivalent to that of a soprano, mezzo-soprano, or contralto voice. The first documents mentioning castrati are Italian records from the 1500s. Joseph Haydn was almost castrated. The last castrato, and the only one of which recordings are extant, was Alessandro Moreschi (1858-1922) who served in the Sistine Chapel Choir. [8]

I wondered for a long time what castrati sounded like until I found Moreschi recordings. It's worth listening to just so you know why they castrated boys.

Apparently, castration is not the end of the world for a male. Life goes on. You can still achieve erections if you get the right hormones, and still have orgasms and ejaculations. A castrated male who doesn't undergo hormone therapy will gradually put on weight around his hips. His nipples become tender and his breasts grow larger. His Battering Ram will atrophy. Hooray for hormones that help, but hormones are a recent development. In the good old days, once your nuts were cut off, you were screwed. I can only think of one benefit of castration. Anyone who kicked a castrated man in the balls would be surprised when it didn't bother him, but I don't think it's worth being castrated for this one benefit!

Chapter 13

Sexual Assault

I often hear about women being raped, but never hear much about males who are sexually assaulted. Lately there are many reports about female teachers having sex with their students. Usually in those cases, the male is underage but often a willing participant. I know I would have been willing during my school years when I had a constant erection and no place to put it.

Men are often unprepared for the fact that they, too, can be victims of rape. Apparently, men are as likely to be raped as females. There must be quite a few aggressive Trout Ticklers out there because one in six men will experience a sexual assault in his lifetime. Statistics indicate that nearly three out of every four men in New Hampshire has experienced sexual or physical violence in their lifetime.[1] There doesn't seem to be a good reason for this, so maybe more men report rapes in N.H. than in other states.

Canada reports that an estimated one in three boys there will be sexually assaulted before the age of eighteen.[2]

Males are less likely to report a sexual assault due to the societal misconceptions about masculinity and sexuality. Male survivors are just as likely to experience post-traumatic stress, depression, suicidal ideation, or will have their experience affect future relationships. How can a man tell anyone he has been raped? I can imagine what it would be like admitting to something like that.

Rape-aXe

Dr. Sonnet Ehlers, a South African woman, invented an anti-rape female condom. Ehlers said in 2009 that she was in negotiation with a company to distribute her product, but it remains unclear as of 2013 whether it has been mass-produced or marketed outside South Africa. She is described as saying with tear-filled eyes that the extreme vulnerability of one rape victim is what sparked her to design this device. The victim looked up at Sonnet and said, "If only I had teeth down there!"[3]

The device is a latex sheaf embedded with shafts of inward facing barbs so it'll stick to a penis like a thousand fishhooks. The women or men would insert it when the possibility of rape arose. Rape-aXe would also help protect the victim from STDs.

Maybe this device would halt many prison rapes. It only seems fair that something so cheap should be given to men going to prison. Many wouldn't use it, but the rapist would never know who wore one and who didn't. A man could stick it in his rectum and if attacked, the assailant's penis would enter the sheaf and be snagged. I think every man sent to prison should be given a supply of these devices, so that if they get raped, the assailant's penis will be hooked like a fish. While the rapist is in pain and trying to detach the condom from his penis, the victim could get the heck away from him. Likely, the condom would remain attached to the perpetrator and could be used as evidence.

Hetero-identification and Rape

I used to think only homosexual men assaulted other men, but I've recently learned that those men in prison who rape other men believe themselves to be heterosexual. They get out of prison and probably continue their heterosexual behavior. They can rape a man or a woman. Evidently, it doesn't make much difference to them. It's often thought that men can protect themselves against sexual assault, but they're as vulnerable as most women. Even tough guys can be taken advantage of by being forcefully drugged or fed enough alcohol so they can't defend themselves. Years ago, I heard of a man going into a bar in Laguna Beach, California and being raped by three men. I never had another drink in Laguna Beach.

Can you name ten reasons a man will turn down sex? Women have a misconception that the answer is zero. They think males always want and are ready for sex of any type. Many male survivors of sexual assault may find themselves asking whether they are heterosexual, gay, or bisexual, and wondering if the assault has influenced their sexuality. Because of societal misconceptions and beliefs, males are "restricted" to a certain array of emotions. Socially, it is quite acceptable for males to express and even act out their anger. It may even seem "healthy" for male survivors to express these intense emotions of anger. If emotional responses are limited, this may result in the suppression of other relevant and valid feelings.

In addition, males are socialized not to show or share their emotions, and are often teased and criticized if they do so. As male survivors of rape, expressing any emotion other than anger may not seem comfortable. Shame is also an underlying emotion experienced by many sexually assaulted men. In our society, males are socialized to be strong, tough, and courageous. However, male survivors may experience shame if they feel that they have not lived up to society's ideas of "manhood." The survivors may also feel shame if they blame themselves for the assault, or if they feel that they could have stopped it. Also, a common feeling of shame may arise if the victim experienced any arousal from the sexual stimulation, even though it's perfectly normal to experience physical arousal during an assault. Many male survivors may interpret this to mean that they enjoyed the rape. Men fall victim for the same reasons as women victims: they are overwhelmed by threats or acts of physical and emotional violence. Men of all sexual orientations and body types can experience sexual assault, but sexual assault does not make the victim any less a "real man."

Chapter 14

A Penis Goes to Prison

I recently received an e-mail from a successful woman writer. She told me that the reason *The Vagina Monologues* became a success was because the author brought up issues that weren't often discussed. Well, I'm asking you, when was the last time you discussed men being raped in prison?

Having spent hours reading about prison rape, I realized that by a slight miscarriage of justice, any man in this country is vulnerable to going to prison. Once he gets there, will he be raped, become a rapist, or will he remain celibate? I thought of a hypothetical situation that could happen to any man:

As I walk home after closing time from the neighborhood bar, a police car stops in front of me. Two cops jump out, each with a gun in one hand and a flashlight in the other, shining the beams directly into my eyes to blind me. One yells "FREEZE" and aims his weapon directly at me. His partner walks up to me with his gun drawn.

"Gotcha motherfucker," he says as he grabs me by the collar and pushes me toward the squad car. "Hands on the hood, and spread 'em." "

You're making a mis—" I try to say, but before I can get any more words out he smashes his flashlight into my mouth.

"Keep it shut, asshole. I'd love to kick the shit out of a rapist," he tells me.

"But I didn't—" I start to say when the flashlight smashes into my head. He hit me so hard the lights go out.

"Now you've fucked up my flashlight, you stupid fuck," he says as I come to.

I knew to keep my mouth shut now.

"Okay Sam, that's enough. This perp's going away for a long time and he'll get what's comin' to him once the gate slams shut. You know what they do to sex offenders in there."

Once I'm booked on suspicion, they have the victim identify me, and unlike the bullshit on TV where they line up suspects with a bunch of similar-looking guys, they might line me up with three or four other men rather than having me sit in a room by myself, if I'm lucky. Even so, in the lineup the other "suspects" are neatly dressed and well groomed. After sitting in a cell for twelve hours, I'm completely disheveled and there's no sink to wash the blood from my face. The victim really doesn't have much choice but to choose me.

The police probably told the victim, "He's already confessed—we just need you to identify him so we can send him where he belongs and he won't be able to do this to any other women." The victim doesn't have much choice but to agree.

Now that they have eyewitness identification, the detectives go to work on me. First they beat me, and then they use psychology to get me to confess.

"You're going away for fifty years unless you confess," the detective says.

"But I didn't do anything,"

"We've got all the evidence we need. An eyewitness who said she hit her assailant in the mouth hard enough to make him bleed, and you're bleeding from the mouth."

"But the cop who arrested me did that."

"Who's going to believe that?" the detective sneers.

"I want a lawyer."

"There's the phone," he says. It's three a.m. and he knew it was highly unlikely I'd get a lawyer on the phone. I try a few numbers anyway and get answering services. While I dial, I wonder where I'll get the money to pay a lawyer. I'd heard how most public defenders do a poor job, but I figure I'm going to ask for one anyway.

"They're all busy right now," the detective says. "One will come as soon as he has time. That probably won't be until tomorrow, though. Look, we've got you dead to rights and you're going away for at least fifty years if you go to trial. Seeing you don't have a record, I can make a deal with you. Sign a confession and you won't do a day over two years."

"No way. I didn't do anything."

"Okay, you go back to your cell and think about it for a while," he says. "Hell, you'll sit in jail for more than two years waiting for trial. Confess now, and I'll try to get you out in eighteen months."

"But I'm innocent."

"So is every other guy in the joint."

I pace back and forth in the small cell, hung-over from drinking cheap booze at the bar before I got arrested, my throat dry as the desert outside the county facility and my head pounding like a sledgehammer. There isn't much heat and no blanket, just a steel cot and a toilet, nothing else. This is a nightmare, but I can't wake up. I figure with a zero bank account, I wouldn't be getting bailed out, and if what I'd heard was true, I'd be lucky to get a public defender that'd stay awake at my trial. I remembered last week when I asked my father for $100. He said, "I'd rather drink it myself than give it to you so you can drink it up. Get the hell out of here and don't ever ask me for money again."

I asked my mother next. After she drew her last $100 out of the bank, she told me she couldn't afford to keep giving me money. The only friends I have sat in the bar all day and could hardly afford to buy a beer, never mind bail me out.

But I'm innocent, I tell myself, frustrated at the thought that the state is willing to spend hundreds of thousands to convict me of a crime I hadn't committed. I recall all the stories of guys who sat on death row for twenty or more years and then are proven innocent. I sure as hell didn't want to spend two years in prison for something I didn't do, let alone fifty years. Eighteen months looked real good by this time, because I knew the cop was right when he said I'd probably sit in jail for two years just waiting to go to trial. I signed the confession and the state's prosecutor told the judge to give me two years. That meant with good time served, I'd be out in eighteen months.

Eventually, the county jail delivered me to the state prison. My first day there was truly a nightmare, and though I tried to imagine it was all a bad dream, it was truly one of the most humiliating experiences of my life. Not only did I have to strip naked and bend over to have my butt probed for contraband, they even inspected the bottom of my feet for whatever I may have been able to hide there. I got my prison clothes and the guards paraded me in front of the other prisoners who hooted and hollered about how they loved new fish. I felt like an animal delivered for slaughter. I was assigned a cell, and as soon as I walked through the door, my new cell mate, twice my size, told me, "If you want to see the sun come up tomorrow you're going to suck my Cramstick."

It's easy to say I'd never participate in that kind of sex, but imagine if I had gotten the fifty years the detective told me I'd get, Pokey would never see a woman again, and that thought was terrifying. Not to mention that my new cellmate threatened to kill me if

I didn't do what he wanted. All this could have been avoided if the original rapist had his temper and his Old Fella under control, but evidently, they were in charge that night.

What would you do in a situation like this? It's worth thinking about. Remember, anyone can end up in prison even though innocent of the charges. It's possible that you or me could end up writing a letter similar to the following:

Inmate's Letter to Human Rights Watch

"I've been sentenced for a D.U.I. offense. My third one.

When I first came to prison, I had no idea what to expect. Certainly none of this. I'm a tall white male, who unfortunately has a small amount of feminine characteristics. And very shy. These characteristics have got me raped so many times I have no more feelings physically. I have been raped by up to five black men and two white men at a time. I've had knifes at my head and throat. I had fought and been beat so hard that I didn't ever think I'd see straight again. One time when I refused to enter a cell, I was brutally attacked by staff and taken to segregation, though I had only wanted to prevent the same and worse by not locking up with my cellmate. There is no supervision after lockdown. I was given a conduct report. I explained to the hearing officer what the issue was. He told me that off the record, "Find a man you can willingly have sex with to prevent these things from happening."

I've requested protective custody only to be denied. It is not available here. He also said there was nowhere to run to, and it would be best for me to accept things . . . . I probably have AIDS now. I have great difficulty raising food to my mouth from shaking after nightmares or thinking too hard on all this . . . . I've laid down without physical fight to be sodomized. To prevent so much damage in struggles, ripping and tearing. Though in not fighting, it caused my heart and spirit to be raped as well. Something I don't know if I'll ever forgive myself for." [1]

Supreme Court Justice Harry A. Blackmun had this to say about prison rape: "The horrors experienced by many young inmates, particularly those who are convicted of nonviolent offenses, border on the unimaginable. Prison rape not only threatens the lives of those who fall prey to their aggressors, but it is potentially devastating to the human spirit. Shame, depression, and a shattering loss of self-esteem accompany the perpetual terror the victim thereafter must endure." [2]

Male Rape

Male on male rape statistics are rarely shown in official reports. In U.S. prisons, male rapists generally identify themselves as heterosexual and confine themselves to non-receptive sexual acts. Victims commonly referred to as "punks" or "bitches," may or may not be seen as homosexual. Punks are a term for those who are generally confined to performing receptive sexual acts. Moreover, though punks are coerced into a sexual arrangement with an aggressor in exchange for protection, these men generally consider themselves heterosexual.

A major concern facing male rape victims is society's belief that men should be able to protect themselves and that it is somehow their fault that they were raped. The experience of a rape may affect gay and heterosexual men differently. Most rape counselors point out that gay men have difficulties in their sexual and emotional relationships with other men and think that the assault occurred because they are gay, whereas straight men often begin to question their sexual identity and are more disturbed by the sexual aspect of the assault than the violence involved. [3]

Many human rights groups have cited documented incidents showing that prison staffs tolerate rape as a means of controlling the prison population. In 2010, according to Human Rights Watch, at least 140,000 inmates are raped in the US each year, and there is a significant variation in the rates of prison rape by race. Stop Prisoner Rape, Inc. statistics indicate that there are more men raped in U.S. prisons than non-incarcerated women similarly assaulted. They estimate that young men are five times more likely to be attacked; and that the prison rape victims are ten times more likely to contract a deadly disease. [4]

Statistics may be unreliable because for every man who reports a rape, there are likely many more that don't report the crime. Here's another estimate. According to a report released by the Bureau of Justice Statistics (BJS) titled "Sexual Victimization in State and Federal Prisons Reported by Inmates, 2007," 4.5 percent of the state and federal prisoners surveyed reported sexual victimization in the past twelve months. Given a national prison population of 1,570,861, the BJS findings suggest that in one year alone, more than 70,000 prisoners were sexually abused.

In 2008 there were more than two million people incarcerated in our nation's prisons. I'm sure the number of sexual offenses increases along with the population. A 2001 report points out that sexual slavery frequently poses as a consensual sexual relationship. Rape victims are often intimidated into feigning consent to sexual activity, to the point of becoming "slaves" and the property of their rapists. Slaves are often identified by holding the pocket of another prisoner.

Prospective slaveholders will sometimes intimidate instead of using violence, and some slaves might not even see themselves as being coerced. Sometimes the enslavement is negotiated as repayment for a debt. [5]

Prison Abuse Begins at Home

An estimated 60,500 state and federal prisoners in the U.S. were sexually assaulted in 2007, according to a national study of rape in prisons. Prison sexuality can be compared to the dominance traits of apes and reveals similar relationship structures. Such animal-like behaviors are widely regarded as an inherent part of human nature. Sexual relationships tend to follow universal archetypes that appear in all aspects of human behavior.

People across America were outraged by the abuses in U.S. prisons in Iraq. A large percentage of Americans think this kind of abuse is unacceptable in any situation. Yet prisoners are subjected to similar atrocities right here at home and we hardly ever hear about it. If you recall, the main perpetrator in the Abu Ghraib prison abuse scandal, Charles A. Graner, was convicted of prisoner abuse. He worked as a corrections officer at Fayette County Prison in Pennsylvania before he joined the army. He learned how to torment prisoners right here in good old Pennsylvania, U.S.A.

The outrage that Americans expressed about this American military prison in Iraq is almost nonexistent toward prisons at home, where prisoners are sometimes treated just as badly, if not worse.

Chapter 15

Fetishes and Stuff

Sexual arousal involves a wide array of possibilities. Psychologists have many names for sex fetishes, and many theories about what causes them. There are fetishes for leather, lace, rubber, and more complicated ones such as infantilism. Infantilism sounds so terrible, I'd better explain that one partner acts like a baby, dresses like one, and is cared for by the other person.

These behaviors are all pretty much caused by He Who Must Be Obeyed, our friend, the Penis. You can name nearly any object or situation and find someone out there who has a sexual response to it. Somewhere down the line, the Strumpet Thumper found that act sexually stimulating, and now requires it to be repeated for its gratification.

Paraphiliacs experience of intense sexual arousal to highly atypical objects, situations, or individuals. Sometimes this reflects a need for an extreme or dangerous stimulus such as a sadistic or masochistic practice in order to achieve sexual arousal or orgasm. In 1986, the Jennifer Levin murder case captivated New York City. The killing in Central Park mesmerized the public with its sordid tales of rough sex.

There are said to be approximately 549 types of paraphilias. I saw a movie years ago starring Peter O'Toole titled "The Ruling Class." In the opening scene, his father, who is a member of the House of Lords in England, is standing on a ladder dressed in a tutu, with a rope around his neck. This was the first time I became aware that such a thing as erotic asphyxiation existed. Around 1,000 deaths a year occur in the United States as a result of asphyxiophilia.

The practice of autoerotic asphyxiation is a fascinating subject and has been documented since the early 1600s. It was first used as a treatment for erectile dysfunction and impotence. The idea for this came from subjects executed by hanging. At public hangings, male victims developed an erection, and occasionally ejaculated during the hanging. The mighty Prince Charming never gives up. The physical pleasure from asphyxia occurs because oxygen to the brain gets reduced, a state of hypoxia that can lead to a semi-hallucinogenic, lucid state.

A more recent case in 2009 involved actor David Carradine's sudden death in Thailand. Officials said he was found hanging with a rope tied around his neck and genitals. Those circumstances have led to speculation that the "Kill Bill" star's death was a case of accidental autoerotic asphyxiation—a death that occurs while masturbating and restricting the flow of oxygen to the brain. Some paraphilia behaviors are harmless, while others, like autoerotic asphyxiation, are dangerous. Peter O'Toole's movie father accidently kicked the ladder he was standing on and hung himself. Something similar likely happened to David Carradine.

Deaths often occur during auto-erotic stimulation when the loss of consciousness is caused by partial asphyxia leading to loss of control over the means of strangulation, resulting in continued asphyxia and then death. Sometimes asphyxiophilia is incorporated into sex with a partner, but others enjoy this behavior by themselves, making it potentially more difficult to get out of dangerous situations. Victims have often rigged some sort of "safety device" that doesn't work the way they had planned before they lost consciousness. In some fatal cases, the body of the asphyxiophilic individual is discovered with genitalia in hand, and sometimes with dildos or other sex toys or pornographic magazines nearby. Sometimes it's determined that the victim orgasmed prior to death. Some individual cases of women with erotic asphyxia have been reported. The mean age of accidental death is mid-twenties, but deaths have also been reported in adolescents and in men in their seventies. Lawyers and insurance companies have brought cases to the attention of clinicians because life insurance claims are payable in the case of an accidental death, but not of suicide.

The composer Frantisek Kotzwara died from erotic asphyxiation. He was a virtuoso double bassist and composer, and is perhaps more famous for the notorious nature of his death. On February 2, 1791 while he was in London, Kotzwara visited a prostitute named Susannah Hill. While in her bedroom, Kotzwara paid her and requested that she cut off his testicles. Hill refused. Kotzwara then tied a leather strap around the doorknob, fastened the other end around his neck, and proceeded to have sexual intercourse with Hill. After it was over, he was dead. His is most likely the first recorded death from erotic asphyxiation.

Susannah Hill was tried for Kotzwara's murder but was acquitted. The court records of the case were supposed to be destroyed. But a copy was used to produce a pamphlet about the incident, including Hill's account of the event. A Prague Radio station was told by a listener that these court records had in fact *not* been destroyed, and had somehow found their way to the Francis Countway Library of Medicine in Boston.[1]

Another interesting autoerotic fatality in Japan concerned a woman, Sada Abe, who killed her lover, Kichizo Ishida, in 1936. She apparently snuffed him during an erotic asphyxiation and then cut off his testicles and carried them in her handbag for a number of days. The case caused a sensation in Japan and is one of the most famous murder cases of all time in that country.

Body Piercings

Body modifications, like ear piercings, have been going on for thousands of years. When the first Neanderthal put a bone in his ear and received some grunts of interest from his tribe, the trend began. Sometimes people are shocked by pierced eyebrows, noses, lips, belly-buttons, and tongue—and piercings in areas that they can't see. Apparently, piercings in erogenous zones are a sexual rush for some people. I looked online at piercing catalogues to get an education about where people get pierced. The penis has eight different locations for a piercing: ampallang, apadravya, dydoe, frenum, guiche, lorum, and Prince Albert. The vulva has only four locations with better-known physiological names: clitoris, clitoral, guiche, and labia inner. In case you're wondering what a guiche piercing is because both sexes have one: it's a body piercing on the perineum.[2]

Piercings are done without local anesthesia as part of the experience. Most piercings in reputable establishments are done under sterile conditions. Since blood-borne diseases are a risk, this is nice to know. But the human skin, unfortunately, cannot be adequately sterilized, so infections are quite common until the piercings heal, but you take the most risk with genital piercings.

Always a Virgin

Here's some good news for the ladies who have a partner obsessed with being their first lover. There's a product on the market that restores virginity — well, almost. At the very least, women can have their first night back any time. All they have to do is insert an artificial hymen into their vagina. It will expand a little and feel tight. When their partner penetrates them, the device will ooze out a liquid that looks a lot like blood. It's easy to use, clinically proven non-toxic to humans, and has no side effects, no pain, and no allergic reactions.[3]

Chapter 16

Angry Penises

Millions of Asian women are missing. In 2005, authorities claimed that the one-child policy in China, from its implementation in the year 2000, had prevented more than 250 million births. As it's now 2013, that figure probably stands at well over 500 million. More women are estimated to be missing in other Asian countries.

Today, roughly 120 boys are born in China for every 100 girls, perhaps the worst gender imbalance in modern human history. Parents can't leave their baby sons unattended without the risk of kidnapping. Boys are so valued that a thriving black market for kidnapped boys exists. Chinese parents prefer boys for many cultural reasons and if a couple doesn't have a boy, they're considered defective in some way.

Female Shortage
Within 15 years, the country may have 30 million men

who cannot find wives. Why should we here in the U.S. care? Imagine 30 million angry penises, distraught because of limited access to a Fur Burger. Consider also that China is growing at a faster clip than any other major nation. China is on course to surpass the United States as the world's largest economy within 20 years. [1]

Maybe the Chinese will get rich enough to buy wives from other countries. That may raise the value of women and help stop female abortion and infanticide worldwide, because they're going to need plenty of wives. Increasing female feticide (abortion) in India could spark a crisis there. Fewer women in their society will result in a rise in sexual violence and child abuse as well as wife sharing. But men don't usually want to share wives. The United Nations says an estimated 2,000 unborn girls are aborted illegally every day in India. This has led to skewed sex ratios in many parts of that country. Now if both India and China become wealthy enough to import women to make up for their shortages, where are all the women going to come from? What if other nations refuse to let their women immigrate to those countries? Throughout history, one way to use surplus men has been to send them abroad to fight wars. The two leading economies, and the two most populous nations on Earth, will justify taking women by force. Might always makes right, history shows.

All these problems are now caused and will continue to be caused because of the High Pressure Vein Cane. That's right, if it wasn't for people thinking having a Staff of Life makes a person better than one who doesn't, there would definitely be more girls in our world than boys. I wonder if these future wars will be called "The Penis Wars?"

I suspect that Trouser Hawgs the world over would rather see more women, not less.

Chapter 17

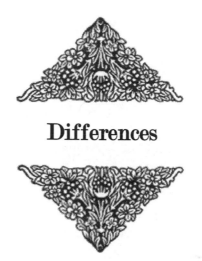

Differences

The main difference between boys and girls is that girls can have babies and boys can help make babies and can pee standing up. Perhaps I should say most boys. I watched Howard Stern conduct a smallest penis contest online and I'm almost certain those guys had to sit down to pee. It took an amazing amount of courage for these guys to strip naked in front of TV cameras and show the world how small their members are. They must have suffered a lot, especially when they were teenagers![1]

Less than one percent of Americans are transgender, a term that can apply to persons who have had gender reassignment surgery or to persons who take hormones or wear clothing and accessories to resemble the opposite sex. It's difficult to fit transgender individuals into rigid legal definitions of what makes one male or female. Transgender rights advocates say that state courts have been silent on whether marriages involving a transgender person are valid. The question is whether it is deceptive or not for a transgender person to live their lives as the opposite gender than the gender assigned on their birth records. A system for how transgender individuals change gender on legal documents is confusing, to say the least. Local, state, and federal agencies have their own standards for defining male or female, and one person's sex may vary from birth certificate, to passport, to medical records. There's no simple answer to the question of how to present legal gender on paper.

States that don't allow same sex marriages are unknowingly performing them. A couple walks into a courthouse, one of them dressed as a woman. They exchange a few words, and within ten minutes, they're husband and wife. Several weeks later, officials may discover that the shapely bride might not have been a woman. The decision to press charges could turn on whether the bride was transgender and identified as a woman, and it is unclear whether the marriage would or could be considered illegal.

The above may sound ludicrous, but when you stop to consider some babies are born with either male or female chromosomal makeup and have both male and female genitalia or with part of the genitalia of the opposite chromosomal sex. Genes don't always correlate to one's perceived sex. Statistics reveal that between 3 million and 10 million Americans are neither male nor female at birth.[2] The medical term for persons of ambiguous gender is "intersexual." There may be millions of XX males and XY females living in the United States today. These are cultural males with male genitalia who are genetically female, and cultural females with female genitalia who are genetically male. Intersexuality in humans refers to intermediate or atypical combinations of physical features that usually distinguish male from female. An intersex organism may have biological characteristics of both the male and female sexes. [3]

The term hermaphrodite refers to a person born with both male and female sex organs. But this is a vague, confusing, and inaccurate definition. There are three labels for hermaphrodites: true, male pseudo, and female pseudo. All are equally genuine. A person born with both ovary and testicular tissue — this person could have two separate gonads, one of each, or a combination of both in one (an ovotestes). The genitalia can vary from completely male or female, to a combination of both, or even an ambiguous-looking organ. The chromosome (karyotype) compliment can be XX (female), XY (male), XX/XY (rare), or even XO (extremely rare). Those XX with female genitalia are raised female (some have even given birth). Those XY with male genitalia are raised male (a few have fathered children). The children born XX/XY or XO (with genitalia male or female are raised in the sex they look most like). Those born with ambiguous genitalia are generally subjected to medical tests so doctors can determine to which sex they should be assigned. Doctors then recommend early surgery to make the child look physically like the sex assigned to them. [4]

I began writing this book to counter some claims made by *The Vagina Monologues,* but during my research, I found that gender differences aren't very clear. This fortifies my point that the sexes need to cooperate on their agendas. Fair treatment for all sexes, male, female, and transsexual, should be the goal.

Chapter 18

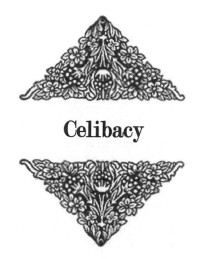

Celibacy

A person who is celibate may be unmarried, single, unwed, spouseless; chaste, virginal, virgin, maidenly, maiden, intact, abstinent, self-denying, or just plain unhappy. A vow of celibacy is a promise not to enter into marriage or engage in sexual intercourse. To be celibate was something I always thought only applied to priests and saints.

Pokey would never allow me to do something like that, nor would any self-respecting Zipper Ripper. But if the small brain has a lapse and the big brain takes over, and logic courses through a man, he can see where he has been led by his member during previous years. Not getting any can be debilitating, but so can some of the things a penis will cause if it's allowed to be in charge.

Where his Slim Reaper has taken him, and what pleasures it has given, must be compared to how much grief it has caused—failed marriages, because the little brain no longer liked his docking space, and prison sentences because it led one to places that were illegal. Not only that, the small brain never stops to think that where it's going may be a dangerous place. Penises have no place in their little heads to store information about STDs. Ignorance is bliss for all Twinkies. Many lead their owners to a pain-filled and sometimes shortened life.

One time after work, I stopped at a bar with my buddies and downed a few beers. A woman came over to where we stood and being half-lit; I reached in and pulled out one of her good sized boobs. "Here Bob, this is for you," I said. But as soon as I put my hands on her boob, Pokey raised his ugly head and demanded some satisfaction. I quickly said, "Never mind Bob, she's coming home with me." When I awoke the next morning and saw what Pokey had dragged home, I was mortified and not wanting my neighbors to see Pokey's handiwork, I asked her if she would please carry out the garbage, so she'd go out the back door. I went out the front and drove to the alley in back to meet her.

Involuntary celibacy is an unwilling state of celibacy. This applies to most guys in prison, and those of us who just don't have what it takes to find companions for our One-Eyed Cow Killer. A Tickle Pickle's thoughts will permeate our brains and lead us to places we wouldn't willingly go. A Taco Warmer will insist that its owner find it a companion regardless of who it is. This is obvious by the lines of cars cruising the areas where prostitutes congregate.

If a man were thinking logically, the last woman he'd think about Dickie Dunkin' with would be a woman of the night. No rational thinking man would want to put his Sugar Stick in an orifice that has been visited by so many Rodzillas before him, leaving their loads and germs behind. Some people are celibate because they have chosen this lifestyle for religious or personal reasons. The idea that large minorities of adults might have little or no sexual contact with others seems incongruous to many people. Yet one researcher found that as many as sixteen percent of married couples had not engaged in sexual intercourse in the month prior to a representative national survey of U.S. residents. [1] Another group of researchers reported that fourteen percent of men and ten percent of women in the U.S. had not had any sexual activity involving genital contact in the past twelve months, and that three percent had none since their eighteenth birthdays.[2]

Celibates were more likely to be introverted and ambitious, and to have parents who married at later ages. In addition, celibate women were more likely to have attained high educational levels and occupational statuses, while celibate men were more likely to be lower class and unemployed.[3]

Spider Man is celibate, and his being a super-hero is a calling that requires a voluntary abstention. With great power comes great responsibility. Evidently, Hollywood takes celibacy seriously. To see moviemakers portray celibacy as a noble, selfless, and even a rational endeavor makes me wonder what they're thinking. If a superhero can't have sex, who wants to be a superhero? I used to think the reason Lois Lane loved Superman was because of his Dong of Steel. But if Superman can't have sex, she must be one frustrated woman, I'm thinking.

There are eunuchs who have been so from birth, and there are eunuchs who have been made eunuchs by men, and there are eunuchs who have made themselves eunuchs by abstaining from sex. Eunuch is such a distasteful word, and when Pokey hears it, he curls up in revulsion. Pokey and I have a constant battle over this subject.

My rational mind was able to gain control during the time I needed to abstain from sex for a period of six months.

I can't say I just quit for six months, a statement similar to a lifelong smoker saying, "Yeah, I decided to quit, so I did." Not that easy and to withdraw from sex is probably more difficult than to stop smoking. I know; I have done both. So I better explain how it happened that I stopped participating.

My wife was infected with the human immunodeficiency virus (HIV). I married her from a compassionate viewpoint to try to make her remaining years comfortable. Didn't work that way, because she wanted to spend her remaining years making me miserable. We parted ways in 1999 when she was attending AIDS group meetings in Las Vegas. There she met men who were also infected, and she felt she could have a better relationship with one of them, so we parted company.

To my dismay, she took our dog Molly with her. I miss that dog to this day, and I have always missed Molly more than my wife. But while married and having sex to keep Pokey happy, my big brain got a toehold because it would thrust images of viruses and germs just waiting to invade my body every time we had sex. Once we split up, I immediately got tested to see if I had been infected. The test was negative, but if infected it could take six months to show up. I did the honorable thing and decided to abstain for the six months so I wouldn't infect some unsuspecting woman.

Giving my big brain six months of control caused it to grow into a powerhouse that Pokey couldn't overcome. Pokey has cried and begged for the last ten years for a companion, but I refuse. I placated him by promising that when I found a woman I was attracted to, he'd soon have company. Recently I met a woman who filled my every criterion plus some. Pokey is excited and wants to meet her, but it has been so long, I'm not sure I know how to introduce him. At the time Pokey was insisting on his God-given rights to socialize with the opposite sex, I had a dream. I went to the airport to pick up a basketball player, famous for the thousands of women he had slept with. During our conversation, he told me how unhappy he was, and wished he never screwed so many women. I think this dream was generated by my big brain to convince Pokey he doesn't need any new friends. But maybe it's a warning from somewhere not to let Pokey have his way.

Appendix A
Penis Names in Prose A-Z

Action Jackson the Alabama Blacksnake is an Apple-Headed Monster, and is my Ace-in-the-Hole. Acorn Andy has an Ass Wedge. Admiral Winky owns an Auger-Headed Gut Wrench for fixing his Albino Cave Dweller.

Buster McThunderstick, Big Lebowski, Bradford and the Pair all want a Breakfast Burrito. Broom Handle and Brutus want a Bulbulous Big Knob, Breakfast Wood. Bush Rusher the Bushwhacker needs a Butterknife for his Bratwurst.

Captain Bilbo the Caped Crusader knows Captain Crook and Captain Hook. Captain Kirk is a Cervix Crusader and a Cave Hunter looking for a Carnal Stump. Chief of Staff, Cherry Poppin' Daddy is a Cherry Picker, and a Cherry Splitter who loves a Chimney Cleaner called Chunder Thunder, who is a Clam Digger with a Clam Hammer.

Dr. Feelgood and Daddy Long Stroke, along with Dancing Cobra the Dependable Bendable Deep Sea Diver looked for a Dolphin called Danger the One-Eyed Ranger who is friends with Dora the Anal Explorer. They wanted Dirk Diggler to help Dangling Participle and Dickimus Maximus find Dingle Dong who is friends with Dipstick. Danglin' Fury used to hang out with Diamond Cutter who is a cousin of Danglin' Wang who knows Dart of Love that lives next door to the Dick of Death. He knows where to find Dickory Dock, who is Danger the One-Eyed Ranger's girlfriend.

Earthworm Jim is Eight Inches of Blunt Fury, and Elastic Plastic is Eight Inches of Throbbing Pink Jesus, and an Early Riser. The Equipment, Elmer the Glue Shooter needed an Ejection Switch for the Elephant Trunk.

Freddy Fish Monger the Fallopian Fiddler met the Fandangled Mandangler at Footlong Fleshbone's place and Fat Finger, Fat Johnson the Fetus Feeler and his Fire-Breathing Dragon brought Fireman Ed and his Family Jewels along.

Girthy McGirth met the Giant-Sized Man Thing at Giving Tree. The Garden Hose Gadget used Grabthar's Hammer to Gash Mallet and the Gearshift Knob's Goose's Neck.

Hunka Hunka Burnin' Love, met Hairy Scary and the Two Bald Men with a Happy Harry Hard-On. Hairy Houdini the Hair Splitter scorned Handfucker and Herman Von Longschlongstein, because Hanging Johnny and Harry Hot Dog told him about Harry and the Hendersons.

Italian Stallion used his Injection Erection to show his Itty Bitty Meat to Impregnator and Intrusion Protrusion at the Ice Cream Machine, and proved Ivan the Terrible was the Incredible Bulk, not Iron Horse.

Jimmy Wriggler held his Jackhammer and hid in the Jack-in-the-Box. Jake the One-eyed Snake used his Jibberstick to Jikipe Jammer, Johnny Cockrane, and Jiminy Cricket.

Kaptain Kielbasa used his Kidney Scraper to remove Kosher Pickle from Kibble 'n Bitz. Kentucky Horn the Kipper Ripper grabbed Ken Cracker by the Kielbasa and King Dong got Kickstand and Knee Knocker to look at his Komodo Dragon.

Longrod Von Hugenstein got Little Bishop in a Turtleneck and his Little Brother to be the Lunchmeat Truncheon. Lord Hardwick chased Lady Dagger with his Lance of Love around the Lap Rope trying to Launch Tower his Leader of the Sack.

Master John Goodfellow and Major Manchowder got Man-sized Manicotti to poke Masterblaster, who was Master of Ceremonies at Murky Lurker, where Moby Dick was Mister Happy. Monty's Python took Mr. Johnson and the Juice Crew to the Muff Marauder and his Molten Mushroom to meet at my Twenty-first Digit.

Nebuchadnezzar the Navajo Hogan and his Nightcrawler got Nail Spike to Nookie Probe Nine-Inch Knocker's Nightstick.

Old Faithful had a One-eyed Blue Vein on his O'Henry. One-eyed Charlie and the Stink Twins had a One-eyed Moisture Missile. Our One-eyed Brother had a One-Holed Friction Whistle.

Panda Express waits for the Pigskin Bus with a Package for Pebbles and Bam Bam. A Pants Snake is known as a Pee-Wee Pajama Python. Penis the Menace and Percy have a Porksicle for Pearl Diver to give to Passion

Pump. Pinocchio grew a Pink-seeking Missile to be a Pussy Plunger.

Quickshot Sam wants a Quarter Pounder and Quivering Member wants a Quarter Pounder with Cheese.

Rumpleforeskin and Rainbow Roll want Richard Head and Ring Stinger to ask Ralph the Fur-faced Chicken if he's the Real Deal. Russell the One-eyed Wonder Muscle thought the Reaming Tower of Penis was Rodney Stickshift. Russell the Love Muscle knew Rogering Ramjet had a Rod Hard Ride on the Rocket to Uranus.

Stretch Johnson the Split-Headed Bishop accused Sacred Scepter of eating his Salami out of the Single Serving Soup Dispenser. Sir Lance-a-Lot took offense and Salty Dog admitted he ate Salami Grande. Squirmin' Herman the One-Eyed German and Spurt Reynolds admitted to Swingin' Dick Nixon that they ate the Sausage Roll.

Tommy Tallywacker the Texas Trout Banger was called a Tennessee Throatwarmer by Thingamabob. Angry as a Twelve-inch Train of Pain, he told Thomas the Third Arm of Justice that Taco Warmer was really a Tickle Pickle and a Throat Choker. Tom Jones, also known as Tom Slick was Thunderstick by Throbbing Horsecock when he and Tiny Elvis saw the Throbbing Purple Spear of Destiny.

Uncle Dick told Uncle Spunk that Uncle Wiggly was the Ugly Brother. Uterus Unicorn cornered Ugly Stick and as an Upright Citizen said Uncle Reamus was an Unemployed Unit.

Vlad the Impaler had a Vaginal Depth Detector and a Vein-laden Meat Pipe. Virile Member said Vicious Dink was a Vomiting Dummy. Veinous Maximus wanted a Vaginal Dilator for his Vagina Explorer.

Wormy McJuicemaker met Wally the One-eyed Wonder Wiener and Wally Whompwacker said Wanker Spanker had a Weapon of Mass Destruction. Whamadoodle wanted Waggerdagger to see the Worm in a Rollneck Pullover. Waldo the Wedding Wrecker, had a Wand of Light called Whisker Slitter.

X-caliber had an XTC Stick, and his Xyster was used for a Xyston.

Yung the Hung sought Yummy Hummer to get a Yard-o-Beef. Yogurt Shooter said, "Yum Yum" when Yogurt Slinger gave him a Yam.

Zipper Ripper caught Zamboni Baloney trying to Zipper Trout. Zamboner the Zapper Wrench grabbed Zizi by the Zoobrick.

Appendix B
Something in Your Trousers

Trouser Hawg wants it all, and can never get enough.

Trouser Mouse hides his face from everyone, but tiptoes across the bed, seeking his hole.

Trouser Snake slithers up and down the leg in search of thrills and who knows what.

Trouser Tortoise is slow to rise and slow to come and slowly becomes the favorite of one and all.

Trouser Flute is a musical creation that trembles in tune when faced with his match.

Trouser Tentmaker always raises his head to show he's there and aware.

Bald Avenger retaliates in the middle of the night and stuffs any hole it can find.

Bald Butler will wait on her hand and foot to rest his head in his favorite spot.

Bald-headed Beauty is actually a scalped penis and doesn't know it's ugly by the world's standards.

Bald-headed Giggle Stick can't help but laugh every

time he sees the spot he's supposed to love, but finds revolting.

Bald-headed Hermit had a hoodie when he first arrived, but someone sold it to a biotech company.

Bald-headed Jesus prays all the time that a companion will soon come his way.

Bald-headed Yogurt Slinger tells everyone his yogurt is the best.

Baldy-headed Spunk Juice Dispenser wants to open a juice stand.

Mr. Eely is as sneaky as a snake and would be related to one if he had two eyes.

Mr. Friendly is always looking for a handshake.

Mr. Giggles is cousin to Bald-headed Giggles and is an apprentice to the Muff Hater.

Mr. Good Bar became famous and he got a big head.

Mr. Happy gets all he wants, whenever he wants it.

Mr. Jiggle Daddy keeps on the move by jiggling around and becoming a daddy over and over.

Mr. Johnson and the Juice Crew know how to find a juicy one.

Mr. Magoo can't see out of his one eye, so he always thinks he's in heaven when he's in hell.

Mr. Matey lived on a ship and loved his mate who had to call him mister because he was an officer.

Mr. Merrymaker celebrates everyday like it's a holiday

Mr. Microphone broadcasts his needs to anyone who will listen.

Mr. Mojo Risin' is charmed right out of his skin when his mojo's working.

Mr. Mouth Missile won't enter just any hole — it has to have a set of lips around it.

Mr. Mushroom Head likes it dark, damp, and wet.

Mr. Pee-Pee is always sticking his head in a urinal.

Mr. Plumpy is fat and soft, and is welcomed in the nicest places.

Mr. Potato Head was once buried in the garden, but was harvested by his owner and now likes everything dirty.

Mr. President wants to lead all the penises in a war against mutilation.

Mr. Rogers invites youngsters to hang out in his neighborhood.

Mr. Salami tells everyone he's kosher.

Mr. Sniffles sniffs everything he gets close to in search of the perfect scent.

Mr. Toad's wild ride ended up in disaster when he found himself in a swamp he couldn't get out of.

Mr. Wigglestick is known for the way he moves around, showing off his abilities to wiggle on his own.

Endnotes

Foreword

1. Dowd, Maureen. "Rape: The sexual weapon." Time Magazine, Monday, September 5, 1983. www.time.com/time/magazine/article/0,9171,926136-2,00.html (Accessed October 6, 2013).

Introduction

1." Museum buys Renaissance erotica." BBC World News, September 8, 2003. http://news.bbc.co.uk/2/hi/uk_news/england/oxfords hire/3119370.stm (Accessed October 6, 2013).
2. "Penis pump judge gets 4-year jail term." USATODAY.com, August 18, 2008, www.usatoday.com/news/nation/2006-08-18-judge-sentenced_x.htm (Accessed October 6, 2013).

Chapter 2 – Blue Balls

1. Warner, Jennifer. "Frequent Ejaculation May Be Good for Prostate." WebMD Health News April 6, 2004. www.webmd.com/prostate-cancer/news/20040406/frequent-ejaculation-prostate (Accessed October 6, 2013).

Chapter 4 – Losing It

1. "Panic in Khartoum: Foreigners Shake Hands, Make Penises Disappear." The Middle East Research Institute (MEMRI), October 22, 2003. http://memri.org/bin/latestnews.cgi?ID=SD59303 (Accessed October 6, 2013).

2. Vaughan. "Koro: A Natural History of Penis Panics." Kuru5hin.org, September 16, 2002. www.kuro5hin.org/story/2002/9/16/81843/6555 (Accessed October 6, 2013).

Chapter 5 – Guns and Penises

1. Carter, Gregg Lee, PhD. "Guns in American Society: An Encyclopedia of History, Politics, Culture and the Law." Santa Barbara, California: ABC CLIO, 2002. Volume 1, p. 477.

2. Paglia, Camille. Salon. "Guns and penises: American society's problem isn't firearms - it's the sexually dysfunctional men and women who abuse them."www.salon.com/people/col/pagl/1999/05/1 2/penises/index.html, May 12, 1999. (Accessed October 6, 2013).

3. ZeldaLily.com. Pasulka, Sasha. "Offensive or Not: The Penis As a Weapon." June 18, 2009. http://zeldalily.com/index.php/2009/06/offensive-or-not-the-penis-as-a-weapon/ (Accessed October 6, 2013).

4. Guns vs. Penis. ItWillPass.com. www.itwillpass.com/guns_remove_every_mans_pen is_to_prevent_rape.shtml (Accessed October 6, 2013).

Chapter 6 – Does Size Matter?

1. The Chartham Study, conducted by Dr. Brian Richards from England in the 1970s. The study was sent for publication to the British Medical Journal as well as the British Journal of Sexual Medicine.

2. "Op can boost size of micropenis." BBC NEWS, December 6, 2004. http://news.bbc.co.uk/go/pr/fr/-/2/hi/health/4071657.stm (Accessed October 6, 2013).

3. Name Your Wang. Zoomdoggle.com, June 10, 2008. http://zoomdoggle.com/2008/06/wang-doggle/ (Accessed October 6, 2013).

Chapter 7 – Penis Enlargement Procedures
1. "Men Worry More About Penile Size Than Women, Says 60-year-old Research Review." Science Daily, May 31, 2007. www.sciencedaily.com/releases/2007/05/070531114303.htm (Accessed October 19, 2013).
2. According to urologist Mr. Manit Arya, Institute of Urology and Nephrology (IUN) in London.

Chapter 8 – Weird Stuff
1. Roheim, G´esa, 1949, "The Symbolism of Subincision." The American Iago 6: 321–328. http://en.wikipedia.org/wiki/Subincision (Accessed October 19, 2013).
2. Stunt Cock. Wikipedia, http://en.wikipedia.org/wiki/Stunt_cock (Accessed October 19, 2013).

Chapter 9 – Penis Fantasies
1. Hall, Allan. November 20, 2005. "World's most infamous cannibal becomes a vegetarian." Daily Mail Online, 2007. www.dailymail.co.uk/news/article-495132/Worlds-infamous-cannibal-vegetarian.html (Accessed October 19, 2013).

Chapter 10 – That's So Gay
1.Autofellatio. Wikipedia, August 30, 2009. http://en.wikipedia.org/wiki/Autofellatio Accessed October 19, 2013).
2. Ibid.
3. Ibid.

4. Penile Plethymograph. Wikipedia, July 16, 2009.
http://en.wikipedia.org/wiki/Penile_plethysmograph(
Accessed October 19, 2013).

Chapter 11 – Male Genital Mutilation
1. The Circumcision Reference Library. "Circumcision is
Cruel Torture." Fleiss, Paul M. *Circumcision*. Lancet 1995;
345:927. www.cirp.org/library/pain/fleiss/ December
5, 2006. (Accessed October 19, 2013).
2. Neocutis.com> Technology, 2004.
www.neocutis.com/modules.php?modid=2
(Accessed October 19, 2013).
3. Athol, A.W. Johnson. "On An Injurious Habit Occasionally Met with in Infancy and Early Childhood." Lancet 1860; 1:344-345.
4. "A Short History of Circumcision in the U.S." Sex-
uallyMutiltatedChild.org. Leo Sorger, "To ACOG [Amer-
ican College of Obstetrics and Gynecology]: Stop Circumcisions." Ob Gyn News, 1 Nov. 1994, p. 8.
www.sexuallymutilatedchild.org/shorthis.htm (Accessed October 19, 2013).
5. History of Circumcision>USA>Circumcision in the
United States of America.
www.historyofcircumcision.net/index.php?option=com_
content&task=category&sectionid=8&id=73 (Accessed
October 19, 2013).
6. U.S. Department of Health and Human Ser-
vices>Women's Health.gov>Female Genital Cutting.
February 1, 2005.
www.womenshealth.gov/FAQ/female-genital-
cutting.cfm. (Accessed October 6, 2013).
7. Brigham and Women's Hospital>African Women's
Health Center>History, April 30, 2009.
www.brighamandwomens.org/africanwomenscenter/de
fault.asp (Accessed October 6, 2013).

8. Stop Infant Circumcision Society>A Short History of Circumcision in the United States. www.stopinfantcircumcision.org/home.htm Leo Sorger to ACOG [American College of Obstetrics and Gynecology]: "Stop Circumcisions," Ob Gyn News, November 1, 1994, p. 8. (Accessed October 6, 2013).

9. Just Sex VLog # 1: Danielle talks about penises - Circumcised vs. Uncircumcised. YouTube.com, February 5, 2009. www.youtube.com/watch?v=CUxZpfc9yXo&feature=Pl ayList&p=3435B48665B0268A&playnext=1&playnext_fro m=PL&index=6) (Accessed October 6, 2013).

Chapter 12 – Castration

1. AbsoluteAstronomy.com. www.absoluteastronomy.com/topics/Castration (Accessed October 6, 2013).

2. Penis Removal. Indopedia.com www.indopedia.org/Penectomy.html (Accessed October 6, 2013).

3. Cendrowicz, Leo. "The Unkindest Cut: A Czech Solution for Sex Offenders." February 11, 2009. http://content.time.com/time/world/article/0,8599,187 8462,00.html (Accessed October 19, 2013).

4. U.S. Department of Justice > Office of Justice Programs > Bureau of Justice Statistics - Criminal Offenders Statistics. www.ojp.usdoj.gov/bjs/crimoff.htm#recidivism, August 8, 2007. (Accessed October 6, 2013).

5. Wikipedia. Castration. http://en.wikipedia.org/wiki/Castration#For_religious _reasons, August 29, 2009 (Accessed August 29, 2009)/

6. "Some members of suicide cult castrated." CNN.com, March 28, 1997. www.cnn.com/US/9703/28/mass.suicide.pm/ (Accessed October 6, 2013).

7. Castrato. Wikipedia
http://en.wikipedia.org/wiki/Castrato (Accessed October 6, 2013).

8. To listen to more of Moreschi's recordings, go to Internet Archive.
http://ia331404.us.archive.org/3/items/AlessandroMoreschi/AlessandroMoreschi-AveMaria.mp3 (Accessed October 19, 2013).

Chapter 13 – Sexual Assaults on Men

1. "Violence Against Men in New Hampshire: A Report from the New Hampshire Coalition Against Domestic and Sexual Violence."
www.nhcadsv.org/Maureen/VAM%20Report%20Final.pdf (Accessed October 19, 2013).

2. The Male Experience of Sexual Violence. University of Alberta Sexual Assault Centre.
www.uofaweb.ualberta.ca/SAC/pdfs/The%20Male%20Experience%20of%20Sexual%20Violence%202009.pdf (Accessed October 19, 2013).

3. Rape-aXe.com. www.antirape.co.za/ (Accessed October 19, 2013).

Chapter 14 – A Penis Goes to Prison

1. Human Rights Watch>No Escape: Male Rape in U.S. Prisons>Preface>Letter from A.H. to Human Rights Watch, August 30, 1996.
www.hrw.org/legacy/reports/2001/prison/report.html (Accessed October 19, 2013).

2. U.S. Supreme Court Justice Harry A. Blackmun, Farmer v. Brennan.

3. Darkness to Light.org > Male Rape. 1997.
www.darknesstolight.org/KnowAbout/articles_male_rape.asp (Accessed October 13, 2013).

4. Prison Rape. Wikipedia, http://en.wikipedia.org/wiki/Prison_rape (Accessed October 19, 2013).

Chapter 15 – Fetishes and Stuff
1. Frantisek Kotzwara. Wikipedia, June 9, 2009. <http://en.wikipedia.org/wiki/Frantisek_Kotzwara> (Accessed October 19, 2013).
2. Guiche piercing. Wikipedia, August 22, 2009. http://en.wikipedia.org/wiki/Guiche_piercing (Accessed October 19, 2013).
3. Gigimo.com>*Artificial Virginity Hymen.* www.gigimo.com/main/product/Artificial,Virginity,Hymen,2299.php?prod=2299 (Accessed October 19, 2013).

Chapter 16 – Angry Penises
1. Grabmeier, Jeff. "China could one day pass U.S. as major economic power, book says." Ohio State University Research News, November 8, 2004. http://researchnews.osu.edu/archive/chinecon.htm (Accessed October 13, 2013).

Chapter 17 – Differences
1. Chrudat.com>Howard Stern: Small Penis Contest. www.chrudat.com/hs_small_penis.html (Accessed October 19, 2013).
2. Intersex Society of North America. "Is it a Boy or a Girl?" www.isna.org/videos/boy_or_girl (Accessed October 19, 2013)
3. CBC Documentaries>The Third Sex: Fact Sheet – What is Intersex? www.cbc.ca/documentaries/thelens/2009/thethirdsex/facts.html (Accessed August 31, 2009).

4. Hermaphrodite Education and Listening Post. www.jax-inter.net/~help/index.html (Accessed October 19, 2013).

Chapter 18 – Celibacy
1. BNET>Health Care Industry>"Involuntary Celibacy: A Life Course Analysis – Statistical Data Included." Journal of Sex Research, May, 2001. Anderson, Sally; Burgess, Elisabeth; Davis, Regina; Donnelly, Denise, and Dillard, Joy. http://findarticles.com/p/articles/mi_m2372/is_2_38/ai_79439406/ (Accessed October 19, 2013).
2. Ibid.
3. Ibid.

About the Author

Joe DiBuduo grew up poor in Boston. He had a troubled childhood and spent time in reform and training schools. As an adult, the house of corrections beckoned him and he spent time there too. A quick turn of fate led him to California and then Chicago, where he married and had children. He spent the next thirty years working as a construction painter, heading wherever the jobs were and working in many states. Joe is now retired and lives in Prescott, Arizona, where he studied creative writing at Yavapai College.

Joe's childhood peers all despised gay people. He thought that attitude was fine until he researched the subject matter for this book. It opened his eyes and he changed his entire outlook on homosexuality and transgender identity. Joe now believes every human has the right to live their lives as they see fit.

Joe became an ethical vegan in 1993, not for dietary reasons, but because he believes humans don't have the right to oppress or abuse other species simply because they are intellectually weaker. He feels human rights and animal rights go together. Humans have a responsibility to care for animals and weaker humans because both are capable of experiencing pleasure and suffering fear and pain. He now finds discrimination on the grounds of species as distasteful as discrimination on the grounds of race or gender.

For more information about Joe's writing, please visit **joedibuduo.com**.

JOE DIBUDUO BOOKS

Made in the USA
Charleston, SC
29 April 2015